THE [7] SECRET TREASURES

THE

[7]

SECRET

TREASURES

A Transformational
Blueprint for a
Well-Lived Life

DR. JOHN DEMARTINI

MEDIA

Published 2022 by Gildan Media LLC
aka G&D Media
www.GanDDmedia.com

FIRST EDITION 2022

Front cover design by David Rheinhardt of Pyrographx

Interior design by Meghan Day Healey of Story Horse, LLC

Library of Congress Cataloging-in-Publication Data is available upon
request

ISBN: 978-1-7225-0594-3

10   9   8   7   6   5   4   3   2   1

CONTENTS

PREFACE
{7}

TREASURE 1
The Secret and Powerful Treasure of
Wisdom, Understanding, Genius,
and Creativity
{9}

TREASURE 2
The Secret and Powerful Treasure of
Business Momentum, Achievement, Fair
and Sustainable Transaction, and Service
{33}

TREASURE 3
The Secret and Powerful Treasure of
Wellness, Vitality, Beauty, and Fitness
{59}

TREASURE 4
The Secret and Powerful Treasure of
Love, Intimacy, Caring Communication,
and Family Dynamics
{79}

TREASURE 5
The Secret and Powerful Treasure of
Social Influence, Leadership, and Legacy
{109}

TREASURE 6
The Secret and Powerful Treasure of
Wealth Building, Financial Independence,
and Philanthropic Contribution
{135}

TREASURE 7
The Secret and Powerful Treasure of
an Inspired Mission, Presence, Equanimity,
and Enlightened Awareness
{161}

ABOUT THE AUTHOR
{187}

PREFACE

In this book, I'm going to discuss your mind, the greatest power you have within you. We'll explore the seven treasures in each of us, such as how to maximize your potential with your body, health, and well-being and how you can have more fulfilling relationships and more love in your life. We're also going to look at your power to lead, because everyone has a natural leader inside, waiting to be born, and that treasure that can be unleashed. We'll talk about developing your financial wealth, because everybody deserves to have prosperity. We'll go into our spiritual nature and how to live an inspired life. Finally, you'll learn about awakening the treasure of your power in business, so you can build your business and do what you love and love what you do. We're going to explore the seven treasures within you and show how you can expand all these areas to live a more fulfilled life.

[1]

The Secret and Powerful Treasure of Wisdom, Understanding, Genius, and Creativity

T

he first treasure that I'd like to share with you is your mind. The power you have inside you is extraordinary. I know this from my own experience: as a child, I was told I would never read, write, or communicate. Later I was able to awaken the power inside me, which was there the whole time, just as it's inside you, although you may not have unveiled it. I'm going to help you unveil that treasure in your mind. The first step is to realize that you already have it.

Everyone has a hierarchy of values. The highest value on your list of values is where your mind is sharp, alert, disciplined, and focused. Areas that are lower on your value system are where you tend to procrastinate and hesitate; you don't remember things; you have a short-term memory there. If we want to awaken our genius and the power of our mind, it's going to be in the area that's highest on our list of values.

We have areas of *attention surplus order* and areas of *attention deficit disorder* (commonly abbreviated as ADD). If you take a child who is labeled with ADD, the teacher will possibly project that label and see the child that way. But in actuality, that child may be able to sit for six or seven hours at a video game, totally focused, and have a photographic memory of that game. This means that the child's higher values are focused on the video game, not on the classes, so the labels that the teachers give aren't fully true. They just don't realize where the child's genius lies.

That genius is inside you. There's a treasure inside you, which corresponds to what you value most. If someone has labeled you as having ADD, know that it may not be fully true, although you may not have discovered your highest value and acknowledged your genius or the power in your mind. The truth is that you do have a highest value and an area where your mind is sharp and alert.

The first exercise that I want you to do is to look deeply and profoundly into your life and find out where your mind is already alert. You know you have it, so don't lie to yourself by saying you don't. Where is your mind most alert? Where is it creative? Where is it spontaneous? Where does it have the power to answer questions quickly? Where does it think creatively?

Don't stop until you find that area. Acknowledge it, write it down, and don't let anybody on the outside impose on you the belief that you don't have it.

When I was seventeen years old, a wise and elderly gentleman changed my life by acknowledging with certainty that I had that power. I hope to do that for you, because I am certain you have it. I've worked with thousands of people all over the world, and although they thought they didn't have that creative genius, I've helped them see where they did. Sometimes they got tears of gratitude in their eyes when they realized it was there. Once they do, they realize that if they want to shift this genius to another area of their life, all they need to do is shift their hierarchy of values. I'll go into that as we move along, but at this point, just know that you have it. Affirm, "I have an extraordinary mind, I am a genius, and I apply my wisdom."

Each of us has different values and different drives. Some are inspired to learn, to devour information. Some are less focused on learning; they want to be more social. Some may want to be more spiritually aware. Others may want to be wealthier financially.

Whatever area of life you want to excel in, I believe it's wise to empower and expand your mind in that area and more. For your mind or consciousness is the core of who you are; and it's your greatest asset. They can take away your arms, they can take away your legs; I have even known people who have had up to nine organs removed from their bodies. Nevertheless, you can still be *you*, because the thing that makes *you* is your ideas and your thoughts, your receptivity to the ideas that come into your consciousness, and the thoughts that come out—your attention and your intention. That's what you are; that's your most powerful creative force. So developing the mind is crucial to maximizing potential in life.

If you look carefully at people in the lower socioeconomic groups, you'll find that they usually have very few books in their houses—maybe a cookbook or a religious text. If you go to the lower middle class, you might find some cookbooks and a few other books around the house. If you go to a middle-class home, you'll find that they have books in the den, the kitchen, the living room, maybe the bathroom. If you go into the higher socioeconomic groups, you'll usually find that they have a library. You can generally see a direct correlation between the number of the books people have in their lives and their socioeconomic status.

I don't know about you, but I have yet to see anybody who gets up in the morning and says, "I want to be less. I want to shrink." There's a yearning inside all of us to expand our awareness and potential. We serve the world by shining, not shrinking, and as a result, we have a desire to expand our mind. If we don't, we constrict our life.

Reading is very valuable, but it's not the only way of gathering information. You can listen to CDs and view DVDs, you can listen to speakers and talks, and you can observe as you socialize: you can learn from people in many different ways. Today you can use the Internet.

Even so, I have found books to very special, because I can take one of the great minds—Plato, Aristotle, Emerson—and read a collection of their thoughts. For a day, or maybe a week, I can stand on the shoulders of these great minds. I believe that you cannot put your hand into a pot of glue without having some of the glue stick. Similarly, you cannot put your mind into the thoughts of great beings without having it leave some greatness behind in you.

If you read something and concentrate on it, some of it sticks with you. You may not be conscious of it, but it's there. Some other time—a day, a week, a month, a year, or five years later—it surfaces when you need it.

When I was eighteen, I was studying everything I could get my hands on, including philosophy and theology. I came across the Greek word *logos*, which meant reason, the field of intelligence, the source of all existence, you might say. The great philosophers were well-versed in many areas, but today we have specialization. The great logos studied by the great philosophers split into the disciplines that we have today, such as theology, cosmology astronomy, mathematics, and chemistry. If you were to study all the disciplines and ologies, you would eventually discover the common threads that make up the logos.

That was my mission. I realized that the average PhD studies about seventy-five to one hundred books in their fields to complete their degree. If you studied that many books in all the different ologies, you could develop an understanding of the logos and find the great common laws of the universe. In order to study the laws of the universe, you want to find what is universal to all the ologies. That was my dream. So I set a goal of reading at least seventy-five to one hundred books in each of the ologies that I discovered. I wanted to find the common thread, the philosopher's stone: the cornerstone of maximizing human potential. I tried to read the works of every Nobel Prize winner, all the great ancient Greek and other cultural authors, all the great philosophers, so as to find the common threads to these disciplines.

Distilling the essence of this wisdom, I discovered that it's all about love, wisdom, and appreciation. When I ask people what would they do if they only had twenty-four hours to live, they almost all say they would communicate their love and appreciation to the people who contribute to their lives. If I ask an audience, "How many of you would love to be loved and appreciated for who you are?" they all put their hands up.

That is the essence of wisdom. Wisdom is the ability to appreciate other individuals and share your love, gratitude and degree of enlightenment with them. All of the disciplines, even physics, chemistry, astronomy, anthropology, and archaeology, lead human consciousness toward that objective.

The next great treasure you have inside yourself is what I call the *reflection principle*. This means that whatever you see in other individuals, you have within yourself.

I've gotten the opportunity to work with thousands of people around the world on this principle, and it's amazing. I had a lady who wanted to be a great consultant to the leading Fortune 100 companies. She had that dream, but she was sometimes intimidated by the CEOs of these companies. Her fear of meeting with them held her back from accomplishing her goal.

I worked with her, and I asked her to identify everything about these CEOs that she admired but which intimidated her. I had her write those qualities down, and then I had her ask herself where she had that same trait in the same or similar form.

She said, "Well, I don't."

I said, "Look again. Don't stop looking."

Because the truth is, if you can see it, you've got it. It may not be in exactly the same form, but there are similarities, and you just keep looking until you fully identify them.

This woman had targeted a particular CEO that she wanted to work with; he was world-famous. She went in and identified where in herself she had the power, the influence, the leadership, the skills, and the knowledge that she saw in him. It took her almost three months to completely awaken to her own form of those qualities, but within a day or so of starting, she was already seeing the shift. In three months, that CEO became one of her clients.

Inside, you have everything you see around you. If you see somebody that has a great mind, you have it yourself. For what you see is a reflection of yourself. You may have been programmed by everybody around you saying that you don't, and you may have believed it for years, but the truth is, you do. The second you start to acknowledge and recognize the form it's in, it consciously surfaces, and instead of being buried treasure, it becomes captured treasure.

Identify one of the most ingenious people that you know. Identify the traits that they have. Then go inside yourself and find where you have them. Don't lie to yourself, saying, "I don't know; I can't." Just dig for the treasure. It may have been hiding there from you for a while, but it's there.

Say that you admire this individual for being quick in decision making. Find out where you have great skills in decision making. It may not be in the same area; it may be the way you raise your family or handle money, it may be in sports or social life, but find out where you have the same capacity as the individual you admire. This will awaken that quality. Sometimes we think other people have a greater deal, but in fact we can have just as great a deal as anybody else.

Go in and dig for your buried treasure. Find out where that skill or mental power is inside you. I myself sat down, made a list of all the Nobel Prize winners, and went through them one by one. I attempted to read some of their works, or at least a biography. I would look into their biographies and log every single trait that I found similar to mine. I thought, "If they have accomplished something in life, I can too. I can go out and do something for the world that's creative and original."

By identifying those traits in myself, my confidence went up; so did the speed of my mind powers. Most importantly, I started recognizing that those traits were there. They weren't lost, they weren't missing; they truly were there. It's amazing what it's done for me in my life. My mental capacities have grown, my visual and audial memory has expanded, my ability to read has gone up; it's been extraordinary.

Go in and discover what you see in other great minds. Where do you have it inside yourself? That's your next treasure, sitting there, waiting to come out.

You have a genius inside of your mind. Do not lie to yourself, saying you don't, and don't let anybody ever tell you that you don't. Dig for it, and you will find it, although you may wear out a few shovels along the way. Just keep probing and digging, and I guarantee you it's there. Find out what form it's in. Nobody's missing anything, but sometimes we don't recognize the form it's in, or we subordinate ourselves to other people, failing to acknowledge our greatness.

I've emphasized the importance of reading, but you are limited in your reading. You may read one book a year, a month, a week, or even a day; nonetheless, the number is finite, and you only have so much time to read and learn. Therefore it is wise to prioritize your reading and identify what you truly want to read. So I say, read the classics, and prioritize what you feed your mind.

I've also found that if you read for thirty minutes a day in a particular area, you can be at the cutting edge of the field in seven years. If you read an hour a day, you could be there in four years. If you read two hours a day, you can be there in about two and a half years. If you could read for three hours a day, you could be at the cutting edge of a field in a year and a half or even less.

This is not just theoretical; I proved it. When I was going to chiropractic college, the instructor was doing a presentation on the brain and said we have more neurons in the sensory and motor areas of our brain associated with our mouth and jaw than any other area.

I thought, "If I'm going to master chiropractic, which is the adjustment of subluxated joints, I need to focus on the temporomandibular joint (TMJ)," which connects the jawbone to the skull. So I went to the University of Texas Dental School and asked the dean of admissions what I needed to study to have a specialty in the TMJ. Assuming I was a dental student, he said, "The bookstore has a list of the curriculums, books, and classes you need."

I bought the books and started devouring them by speed-reading (by that time, I was learning how to speed-read very rapidly). A few months later, I went to a New Year's party at a dentist's house. He asked, "What are you doing presently?"

I said, "I'm studying the TMJ."

We started a conversation. He said, "I have a study group. Can you come and present to my study group what you know about TMJ?"

I said, "Certainly." So I came to this group at his home, and although I was a first-year chiropractic student, I gave a presentation for an hour and a half to about twenty dentists.

After I got through, they said, "Would you have more information?"

"Absolutely." I came back the next week, the next week, and the week after that. For nine months, I presented TMJ information.

During that time, a gentleman in the group said, "I've got a group called the Southwest Craniomandibular Society. We'd like you to have you speak at this group."

As a result, I got to speak on TMJ to two hundred dentists in this group. Shortly afterward, someone asked, "I have a four hundred member dental association; it's large, it's basically all of the dentists in this region of Texas. Would you like to speak to this organization?"

"Great," I said.

Shortly after that presentation, I got an opportunity to speak at the American Dental Conference with the three top TMJ specialists in the world. All of this took place in somewhat less than two years.

If you concentrate on a specific subject to this degree, and then you widen your perspective and start linking it gradually to everything else you can continually broaden your expertise. So I started studying questions like, how does TMJ relate to the development of human consciousness? How does it develop in our embryology? How does it affect our nutrition?

If I were to study four times faster, I could do four or more PhDs or doctorates during that same time, and I thought I could do that. So I started studying astronomy and lectured at Rice University and University of Houston on two evenings on astronomy. I did something similar with oncology. I realized that the mind is not limited, except by the limits we impose on it.

The next great treasure you have inside you is the power to ask questions. In fact, the quality of your life is based on the questions you ask.

I want to go through a few of the questions that you might want to ask yourself. If you do and write down the responses, you'll probably be amazed what's going to come out of you.

The first one is, *what would I absolutely love to do in life?* When I was younger, I asked myself this question. The answer that came was that I would love to travel to every country on the face of the earth and share my inspirations with people. That's what I wrote.

Ask the question. It doesn't matter whether you initially think you can achieve what you come up with; asking that question kindles a fire in your heart. In the depths of the earth, where treasures are hidden and where great diamonds are born, there's a geothermal power and pressure. Everybody has within them that same power to burst forth and explode with possibility.

So go in and ask yourself, what is it that I would absolutely love to do in life?

The second question is, *how do I get handsomely and beautifully paid to do what I love?* If we allow ourselves to do what we love and get paid for it, our vocation can be our vacation. Ask questions that enable you to do what you love and be rewarded for it, so your actions and your rewards are correlated. That way, you can live an inspired life.

When you get an answer to this question, you may initially think, "I don't know. I can't possibly do that." Yes, you can. I've asked these questions of thousands of people, and I've made them write down their responses. They have suddenly had light bulbs go on and said, "Oh my God, I could do this."

Make sure to take out a pencil and paper, or your computer, and write down the answers to these questions: *What would I absolutely love to do in life? How do I get handsomely and beautifully paid to do it?*

The next question: *what are the seven highest-priority and most important action steps that I can do today to move me one step closer to making that goal a reality?* Because if you take even little steps towards your goal every single day, sooner or later it unfolds. It's a matter of chopping things down from big projects to small bites. If you take a little baby step every single day, you gradually build momentum, and all of a sudden you have mastery.

I spoke with a lady in Quebec City, Canada. I asked her to answer those questions, and she said she couldn't come up with anything. I said, "Look again; keep looking; keep digging." All of a sudden, with a tear in her eye, she said she got an idea: "I love to travel the world, and I love dancing. I would love to get paid to dance. But I don't know how I could."

We brainstormed for a moment, and all of a sudden, she realized she could gather a group of people together from her dance studio and take them on a trip to Spain. She could find one of the greatest flamenco dancers and have her group learn from that dancer. She organized about fifteen people to pay thousands of dollars to go on a tour, see the sights, and dance throughout the evening, learning from one of the great masters. She filled that tour up, and I think she netted about $4,700, just because she learned to ask and answer those three questions. Now she had a business taking people on dance tours.

No matter what your truest objective or dream is, it's possible. I'm amazed what happens when people ask those questions. During my seminars, people come to me with extraordinary stories about what they have found.

Once you've got those seven action steps, you might ask, *what obstacles could interfere with that goal? How can I solve them in advance?* It's wise to have a preemptive game plan in advance. Ask, "What if this happens?" Think of what could be and how you would deal with them. With a plan, you're not reacting; you're acting. As you've heard, people who fail to plan, plan to fail. When you have some foresight, obstacles are no problem. You just keep going towards your dream.

The next question to ask yourself is, *how can I do whatever I'm doing more effectively and efficiently? How can I more effectively act towards my dream?*

The last question is this: *no matter what has happened along the journey, whether supportive or challenging, whether perceived as nice or mean, how did it serve me?* If and when you can answer this, instead of feeling friction and frustration, you'll become fueled.

By asking these quality questions, we get a different life. I started doing this many years ago, and I live an extraordinary life today. I'm blessed today because I learned how to manage my mind and ask these questions.

As I've said, you have great treasures in your mind, but you may not have unveiled them. One of the greatest treasures is the ability to ask quality questions—the ones that inspire you—and find solutions to obstacles that you perceive may interfere with your inspirations. Ask those questions, and watch what happens.

As a professional speaker, I've been traveling many years. I've asked myself, "How can I speak at the Great Pyramids of Egypt? How can I speak at the Great Amphitheater in Greece? How can I speak along the Great Wall of China?" From asking those questions and following the steps that I've just outlined, those things have come true in my life.

Don't underestimate the power of the questions you ask yourself. Extraordinary questions lead to extraordinary results—which you deserve. There's a buried treasure inside you: the questions that you ask. Take time to unveil them, dig them out, and add them to the other treasures in your mind.

Imagine reaching out with your hand and grabbing this treasure now. Visualizing with your mind's eye, I want you to imagine yourself exactly how you will live your life today.

At first, you may have a little bit of haziness and it may be a little awkward, but I want you to dig and clarify in your mind exactly how you would love to live your life today.

I'm a retired chiropractor. When I had my practice, I would sit in my office before starting my day, and I would close my eyes. I would visualize all of the patients coming in. No matter what their concerns or problems were, I imagined them somehow finding a solution and having healing.

I can't explain the power of this practice: but you will be grateful once you have experienced it. I watched so many of these visualizations come true. I imagined patients coming in and asking questions and making statements to me and me answering. That same day, those people would ask those very questions. I would get a tear in my eye, thinking, "Oh, my God, this is amazing—the power of the mind when we visualize."

We can create our outcomes. I call it the power of intention. Whatever we have in our heart that we would love to create in life, if we can visualize it and focus on it in ever finer detail, we can help it become reality. This is how Tiger Woods created his great golf scores. This is exactly how great sports people like Michael Phelps reach their goals: they can see them in advance in their minds.

You know you have a vivid vision when you are able to articulate it to yourself or others perfectly clearly and smoothly.

Your vitality soars, and you have enormous power. In fact, the vitality in your life is directly proportionate to the vividness of your vision.

Your mind has the capacity to visualize things in such detail that I believe it affects the quantum fields that surround you and permeate the universe. It alters the people, places, things, ideas, and events in your life and brings your desire into reality. I believe that we are made with the power of such creativity, and we have extraordinary capacities inside us. It is simply up to us to apply them.

Visualization is one of our greatest capacities. If we honor ourselves with a great vision, hold that vision, and not lose sight of it, it can generate enormous creative power.

When I was a child, I had learning difficulties. When I was seventeen, I met a great teacher. He gave me the opportunity to go through this kind of meditation experience. I saw a vision of myself speaking. At the time, that was the last thing that I ever imagined would show up in my mind. But it did, and it was so vivid, so clear, that I was there; I became one with the vision. In that moment, it was as if I were speaking to a million people. That picture has been with me ever since; it has inspired me; it has brought tears to my eyes.

That vision, which I have held since I was seventeen, is now reality. I'm living exactly the life that I saw. You are capable of doing the same, although you may have been afraid to allow that vision to come out. You may have let the fears of life stop you. You may have let perceived authority tell you can't do it. You may have thought you would fail or wouldn't be able to make a living doing what you envision. You may have been afraid that you would lose loved ones or be rejected. You may have thought you didn't have the mental or physical capacities. But the truth is, if you have a vision, you have the capacity to create it, even though you may require occasional assistance along the way.

Visualize how you want your life to be. Cut out pictures of the things that you'd love to create in your life, and create a storyboard of how you would your life to be. I have a book containing every one of the visions and dreams that I have had, and I carry it with me on my computer. I cannot tell you how much that's impacted my life and the people that I have shared it with.

Visualize your life the way you want. Once it's clear in your mind, articulate it, write it out, and affirm it as if it's real today.

When I was seventeen, I was not considered a genius. I was a high school dropout; I had learning difficulties. I had never even read a book from cover to cover. But the gentleman I'm talking about, Paul Bragg, told me to say to myself each day that I am a genius and that I apply my wisdom. He told me to repeat my affirmation and vision for every single day for the rest of my life and visualize what it might look like. As a result, it unveiled, and it drew out of me something I didn't even know I had inside, just as it will do for you. If you dig inside yourself and affirm and visualize exactly how you want your life to be, you will move in that direction.

You cannot plant flowers in the garden of your mind without having them grow. To override any weeds of doubt that may come in, focus on how you want your life, and watch what happens.

When I was moving to my second office. I visualized the dream office in my mind. Lo and behold, it showed up. To this day, thirty-six years later, I have the dream office that I had visualized.

Visualization is powerful. No matter what you see, use it, because its power lies in action. Close your eyes, visualize exactly how you want your life, and watch the creative mental power inside you, the power of intention, start to emerge.

The power of visualization works if you apply it. Know that your innermost dominant thought becomes your outermost tangible reality. Visualize, think of, and affirm exactly how you want your life instead of how you don't.

I learned this from an episode of *The Twilight Zone* when I was a young kid. It was about a guy whose brain would get bigger and bigger every time he read a book. After a while, he started speed-reading books and scanning through libraries; as he was absorbing all of it, his head continued to get bigger.

That's what I visualized. I visualized myself walking into libraries and absorbing information. When I fly over cities, I imagine all the libraries and see myself absorbing the information in them. Why not use your mind and your visualization? Visualize what you want and how you'd like to do it, and know that those visions will flourish.

When I was seventeen, I had that vision of standing up in front of a large group of people, and I've held it to this day. And year after year, the numbers of people that I speak to keep growing.

What do you want to say to yourself? How do you want to talk to yourself? What do you want to see for yourself? See yourself being awakened and having incredible capacities to learn. Say to yourself, "I'm a master reader. Whatever I read, I retain, I'm a master retainer; I absorb everything. When I need it, it's there."

What would happen if you gave yourself permission to awaken your genius? I believe that's one of the powers of life: we're here to awaken our mental genius. A genius, as I define it, is one who listens to the inner voice that prompts them and follows their inner vision. They may have the whole world against them, they may be ridiculed or violently opposed, but they let nothing keep them from that vision. If that voice and that vision on the inside are greater than the opinions on the outside, eventually the opinions on the outside will follow the vision on the inside.

[2]

The Secret and Powerful Treasure of Business Momentum, Achievement, Fair and Sustainable Transaction, and Service

Everybody would love to feel successful. That's one of the great treasures: to have success and fulfillment. But I'd like to break some new ground here and show you something that you may not have thought of before.

One time a doctor came to my office, and he wanted to consult with me. He said, "Dr. Demartini, I need to hire you to help me become successful."

"Great," I said. "Tell me a little bit more."

"I'm in practice, and I'm not doing as well as I'd like. I'd like to have a bigger practice."

"Great. So where are you currently successful?"

"Dr. Demartini, you're not hearing what I'm saying. I'm not successful, and I want you to help me be successful."

"Great. So where are you successful now?"

"Dr. Demartini, you're not listening. I'm not. I want to be. That's what I'm here for."

"Great. I understand. So where are you successful in your life?"

"But I'm not."

"Yes, you are. I want you to look again. You already have success; your success is in accordance with the highest values on your hierarchy of values. Look carefully. Where do you have success in your life? Look carefully in the area of life that is truly most important to you."

"Oh, yeah. I guess I do have a relationship with my wife that's quite amazing. We've been married about ten years. I guess that's really successful."

"Where else do you have success?"

"I guess I have a great relationship with my son. He's on the baseball team, for which I'm the coach, and we may win the pennant this year. We have a really close relationship."

"Where else are you successful?"

"We all work in our yard, and we are hoping to get yard of the year in our community. We might. We're working together towards that."

"Where else are you successful?

"My mother-in-law lives with us. Most people don't get along with their mother-in-law, but we have a great relationship. I guess that's successful, because that was a goal."

"Where else you are successful?"

"I assist at the church and sometimes give little classes. That was a goal I had."

"Can you see that you have successes in your life?"

"Yes."

"Now in order to feel like a failure, you must be comparing your success to somebody else's. So whom you are comparing yourself to?"

"I guess I'm comparing myself to this doctor who lives up on top of the hill. He's got a big house and nice cars."

"OK. This doctor up on the hill—how's his relationship with his wife?"

"They're having some challenges."

"What about his kids?"

"One of his sons is on drugs, and they're having problems with him."

"What about their yard?"

"I don't think they even go into their yard. They don't pay attention to it, because they're so busy. They just have people to take care of it."

"What about the mother-in-law?"

"I think they moved out of state to get away from her."

"What about church?"

"I don't know if he even goes to church. I don't know if that's his focus."

I said, "Can you see that this man has one set of values and you have a completely different set? Therefore you have different areas of success in your life."

"Well, now that you pointed it out, yeah."

"Would you sacrifice yours for his?"

"God, no."

"Well, then, realize that's why you have what you have. Your values have led you to your form of success. But sometimes when we go through life, we minimize our form of success and think that somebody has a better form. That's not to say that we can't expand our forms of success or enjoy some of the things they have. It just means that we don't want to downplay our own successes, minimize ourselves, and subordinate ourselves to other people."

This gentleman looked at me with a watery eye and said, "I didn't realize I had that. Now that I think about it, I really would rather have what I have. But is there any way I can grow my practice, even though I wouldn't want to sacrifice my family life for it?"

"I really appreciate that," I said. "That's why you have what you have. You've made sure that you've earned enough money to take care of all the things that really important to you. But if you'd like to grow your practice, I can give you tips on that. I can give you some ideas on how to grow a business."

At that point, instead of beating himself up, he started to honor his success.

Please—whatever you have in life, honor that first. When you're grateful for what you've got, you get more to be grateful for, but don't think that it's missing in the first place. As I've already emphasized, nothing is missing; it's just in a form that you may not be acknowledging. Your hierarchy of values is dictating your destiny. As your values change, your destinies along your journey in life also change.

Your success is already there. That's the secret treasure you want to grasp first. You really have success; your actualized potential is already there. Don't minimize it, don't think you've got to get it; it's there. If we'd like to transform it, let's go for it. I'm going to give you the keys to the business success that you'd like and maybe to wealth.

Again, your hierarchy of values dictates the form your success, or failure, comes in. Don't envy other people or put them on pedestals. Envy is ignorance, and imitation is suicide. If you put these people on a pedestal, you inject their values into your life; you're attempting to live their values. When this goes against your own values, you will require outside motivation to keep you disciplined. That's because you're not honoring your own highest values. When you honor your higher values and love yourself for who you are, you awaken your own true success, whatever that may be. Once you realize you already have success, as the gentleman above did, then, if you'd like to change its form, all that is required is to change the hierarchy of your values.

All this said, how do you change your form of success? At this moment, you may be working for somebody else, but you have an inkling about a dream business in the back of your mind. You may be starting on your own as an entrepreneur. You may already be successful. Still, pay careful attention, because these secret treasures will serve you.

If you don't know what you're going to do with your business, its vision and mission, or your desired outcome, you're not going to manifest success to the degree that you could if you have a crystal clear vision of where you're going. That's one key element of growing an amazing business.

I've consulted with entrepreneurs who have come to me and said, "I want to grow the business, but I've plateaued. I just can't seem to break through."

I say, "Where are you going with it? Where are you taking the business?"

"I'm not sure. I just know I want to grow it."

"What does that look like?"

"To double the market."

"That's vague. What does that mean? What specifically are you doing? What service are you going to offer, whom are you going to offer it to, and when are you going to do it? Where are you going to do it. Why and how?"

If you don't ask the who, what, when, where, how, and why questions, you won't get clear about where you're going to take your business. It will flounder and wander all over the place.

By the way, if you want to start a new business, unless you make a plan and get really clear about it, you're not likely to make it happen. And if you don't think about your plan deeply enough to make it detailed, any detail you leave out will become an obstacle.

So the first secret is to get clear about where you want to take your business. The clearer you are, the more vitality the business has. You can't put the soul back into your business's corporate body without a clear vision. That takes clarity on the "soul" level.

Go inside yourself, activate your inner voice and vision, and get clear about what you're going to do. What service are going to provide? How are you going to do it? When you're clear about your mission, you'll have a message that you will be able to filter down to your employees and clients.

Clarity will save you hours of work. Working on your business pays more dividends instead of merely doing the same thing while expecting different results. So go into it and get clear.

Often people just gaze superficially at their business and expect fantasy outcomes. When I'm building my business in my mind, I visualize myself setting foot in every country on the face of the earth. I see myself going into the great hotels and great convention centers and appearing on the media. I see it in my mind, and it manifests.

Focus, focus. Clear, concentrated energy draws opportunity, but you will not stay focused if your chief aim or purpose doesn't align with your highest values. If you do not have a high value of building a business or offering a service, you'll keep frustrating yourself, because you'll keep going off on other actions that are more important to you and distracting yourself from your business. If you really want to build a business, be clear about it, and make sure it aligns with your highest values. That way you'll be inspired, because when you can't wait to get up in the morning to go to work, people can't wait to get your service.

If going to work is not inspiring you, you might want to move on to something else. If you're not inspired, you're holding back the company you're with.

I was in Las Vegas doing a presentation, and afterward I went to see Celine Dion perform. Before she started to sing, she said something very important: "Everyone on this stage, every day, does what they love and loves what they do. Everybody here loves to perform, dance, and sing, and this is my greatest dream: to be up here and perform for you. Don't sacrifice your life by doing anything less."

To me, that's what it's about. If your heart and soul are into your work, I can almost guarantee you that your business will thrive. There's no way you can be enthused and go to work without having more business come to you.

Be clear about your mission. Be clear about your goals and objectives. Make sure they align with your highest values. Make sure to express them clearly to all the people that are working for you. If you're working for somebody else, start doing that within the business you're working for. That way you'll get promotions, opportunities, or the courage to start your own. But don't go to work and be a deadweight; don't be mere overhead. Get out, and go on to something greater. Do something you love, and be clear about what you want to offer.

I had the opportunity to speak at IBM in Houston. About 75 percent of the people present were not inspired; I was there to help them get inspired about their job. After I got through speaking, some people decided to give notice and move on. The others decided to get focused, and the company grew as a result. That's exactly what will happen in your company if you are inspired and have a clear mission and vision.

Know that the secret treasure is waiting inside. If you're inspired and let it out, amazing things can happen. We are here to serve. We're here to rake in the rewards of all the diamonds that we glimmer with.

I have long said that the world is my home, and every country is another room in a house. I will do it whatever it takes, travel whatever distance, and pay whatever price to give my service of love. I'll set foot in every country in the face of the earth until I've succeeded. That's my value system, so that's what's has showed up in my life. I believed that I would attract the appropriate people, places, things, ideas, and events. I believed I would be at the right place at the right time to meet the right people to make that vision happen. And that is what has happened. I have now spoken in one hundred and seventy countries to date. Those that lose the vision perish; they go off on tangents, restart, and then rebuild. Those that hold the vision and persevere will flourish. Our innermost dominant thought becomes our most tangible reality, so they change the quantum field. The quantum field is trying to equilibrate the mind and make it grateful, certain, loving, and present. The matrix of love is on this earth. The field of consciousness is trying to help everybody live true to themselves.

When I studied brain research, I saw that the brain is trying to do this very thing for people. I saw the same thing when I studied psychology, business development, ecosystems, ecology, and sociology. They're all pointing to helping people maximize their potential, but we don't see it. Everything that is going on around you acts as a feedback for you to be the most authentic and inspired you.

Today you may want to kneel on the side of your bed like a child and humbly say, "Dear Universe, Dear God, Dear Source, Dear Inner Soul, Dear Authentic Self, reveal to me what I'm here to do." Don't stop until you get clear. To this day, I still do this. If you humble yourself to that ordering field, the voices will turn into *the* voice. When that inner voice and vision are greater than all opposition and opinions on the outside, you've mastered your life.

Just as plants grow to the sun, so do people grow to levels of enlightenment. If we enlighten ourselves by acknowledging our magnificence, people will be magnetically drawn to us, because we're also giving permission to others to live life truly. If you're doing that in a business, you can't stop it from growing.

When I hire people for my business, I have a little exercise. After we've gone through the usual details of their job skills and background, I ask people what they would do with $10 million. Sometimes I actually write a check to them for that amount and show it to them. I ask, "If I were to give you your first check for $10 million and you never had to work another day in your life, what would you do?"

This completely throws the candidates; they're baffled. They drop any façade they came in with and talk about what they really love to do. If what they say doesn't match exactly what I'm hiring for, I say, "Thank you very much. That'll be all," and I move on. I've learned that if you get somebody who is not inspired about their job, you end up adding costs into your business instead of productivity.

I used this process on one lady. She didn't even know all the things that I did, but her dream, history and skills matched the job description that I was hiring for. She worked for me for nearly two decades until she passed on, and she did an amazing job. She's was director of my company.

If you take on a job that doesn't inspire you, you're not as likely to help the company; you're just doing your job out of security and fear. And if you're hiring somebody who's not really inspired by the job, you're just adding to the weight of the company.

Years ago, I was hiring a manager for my practice. One gentleman walked into my office with a briefcase. He was about fifty years old.

"Dr. Demartini," he said, "I am the man for the job. I know I can manage it."

"Oh, great." I wrote a check to his name for $10 million and gave it to him. He looked thrown off.

"What would you do with your life if you had $10 million and didn't have to work anymore?" I asked.

"I know what I would do," he replied. "I love carving, woodworking, and making furniture."

"Thank you so much. I appreciate the interview. That'll be all."

"Is that the interview?"

"That's all."

"Are you going to hire me?"

"No."

"Why?"

"Very simple. If you're such a great manager and you would love to be a woodworker but you haven't figured out how to manage your own life to be one, why would I expect you to be able to manage my company?"

Humbled, he looked down and said, you know, "Dr. Demartini, that's a great question you just threw at me. You're absolutely right. If I haven't managed my life, it's expecting a lot to be able to manage your whole company."

He shook my hand and walked off.

Three weeks later, he came back to my office and asked if he could meet with me again. He had a paper bag. He said, "Dr. Demartini, you changed my life three weeks ago. When you asked me that question, you made me think deeply. I've been looking for a job for three months now and haven't found one. I thought, what have I got to lose? Why don't I try starting the company of my dreams? Why don't I go ahead and start to create a business making furniture?

"So I started telling people about it. Lo and behold, I got a customer right off the bat. I'm making some furniture for him, and I'm in business. I want to thank you, because I would never have done it if it wasn't for what you said.

"When I was in your office last time, I saw the coloring and grains in your woodwork. I noticed that you had Kleenex boxes on your counters, but they weren't covered. Dr. Demartini, I'd like to offer you a gift in thanks for what you've done for me." He had created beautiful Kleenex holders that matched my woodwork. "I would love to install these for you," he said. "I just want you to remember me, because you inspired me."

I want to remember that myself. This man confirmed the importance of refusing to settle for anything than what you would truly love in your life. You may be in a job right now that may be not inspiring. Keep your eyes open, focus, and start planning and designing how you really want it. Mediocrity is not the way to live your life.

That doesn't mean to dump what you're doing now and go out to take wild risks. It means start planning now. If you fail to plan, you plan to fail. Start planning now exactly what you really want to do. Transition from what you are uninspired by to what you are spontaneously inspired by and watch what happens—your vitality will soar.

Doing what you love will give you an enormous burst of energy. I believe that we're made with a brilliant light inside us. We can light the path of others and give them permission to live lives and have careers they deserve. I want you to know that you deserve to do what you love and love what you do.

Once you have a planned strategy in place, it's wise to put a functional structure in place. Who's going to do what? What functions are needed to fulfill your mission? Then place people into those functions. Create an organizational chart of exactly who and what's going to be necessary to get that that job done.

Once you have the organizational structure in place, put in the responsibilities: I need somebody who does research; I need somebody who types; I need someone to produce books; I need somebody in promotion, somebody who takes care of the finances, flight arrangements, and so on. Once I have the positions that are needed to fulfill my mission, I find the people to fill them.

If you have a job that's not inspiring, I'll show you how to make it inspiring. Make a list of everything you do in your day at work. Write it all down—things you like, things you dislike, things you're frustrated by, things that are tedious. Make this list on the far left column of your page.

On the far right side, write down the mission and objectives of the company you work for. If you don't know, go to your manager or superior and ask, or look it up on the Internet.

In the middle column, write down the seven most important things in your life: true dreams and goals that you're working towards—your mission, what inspires you.

Once you have those three columns, do the following. Between column one and two, next to each of your job activities, write down how each activity helps you fulfill your objectives.

Take something that's frustrating or tedious. Ask this question: "How will that activity help me fulfill my dreams, my objectives, and what's most meaningful for me?"

At first, you're going to say it doesn't; that's why you call it tedious. But believe me, it's not what you do, it's how you perceive it. Look at the task again. Know that anything that happens in your life can help you fulfill your mission. Look more deeply than you've ever looked before. Don't give up; don't give yourself excuses; answer this question. If your highest value is raising a lovely family or saving money for education, how will doing that specific activity help you get it? Write down not just one answer, but a minimum of ten. Twenty is even better.

I've done this exercise in companies around the world. People think they can't do it at first, but once they start probing, they say, "Oh my God, I can," and they write down ten or twenty ways in which that activity helps them fulfill their highest values. They link those activities to their heart, their brain, their highest values, and what's meaningful. Suddenly the task is no longer tedious. Once the brain sees how they're getting what they want, they're going to work for themselves, not for the job. Nobody goes to work for the sake of a company. They go to work to fulfill their highest values—what is most meaningful to them.

Do that one by one, down your list. If you do it thoroughly, writing ten or twenty answers for each task, the frustration of that job will subside. Now it's lighter, and you look more forward to go to work.

I know this process takes some work, but a few hours spent on it will save you enormous amounts of energy and time. It will allow you to love what you're doing temporarily while developing your plan to do what you truly love.

Once you've gone through this process for every one of your job activities or responsibilities, ask and repeatedly answer this question: "How specifically is fulfilling the mission of my current company helping me fulfill my highest values or my long-term mission?" If you do that, you will find out that fulfilling the mission of the company is also serving you. It's a transition, if nothing else. It's giving you tools, leads, opportunities, skills.

Don't be so blind as to think your job is not serving you. Find out how it does. Dig in, and make those links and associations. Come up with fifty or one hundred ways in which serving that company serves your life.

If you link your job description to the most meaningful values in your life, and you link your company mission to these same values, your job will become more inspiring. You'll have more free energy; you'll have more vitality; you'll get up earlier in the morning. You won't be as frustrated and drained at the end of the day. You'll bring more love and appreciation to your family; you'll tend to eat more wisely and won't be depressed. You'll feel more socially interactive with the people at work, because you'll see how they're serving you.

As you're doing this process, if this job is not part of your long-term vision, then start your plans for that vision. But be thankful for this job, because it's still helping you get toward your dreams. It is *on* the way, not *in* the way.

It's not what happens to you; it's not even what you do. It's how you perceive things. You have the power to perceive your job differently. That's the greatest gift: your mind has the power to transform your perceptions of your career. You have the power to change it. You also have the power to transform and build the career of your dreams. Make those links; take the time, it's worth it; you're worth it. Say to yourself, "I'm worth the transformation. I deserve to do what I love and love what I do."

Watch what happens. This activity will electrify the secret treasure of your own brilliance. I can almost guarantee that if you do it, you'll take it to other people in your company, even to your family, because they may not be loving what they're doing. You deserve to share that. Share it with them, share it with yourself, and watch the difference.

When you find somebody who's got a dream to do what you want them to do, give them the opportunity to be trained. Don't just dump them into the job without training. If you don't train them, you may not be able to effectively delegate. If you can't delegate, you're stagnant.

Streamline what you're doing. Make a list of everything you're doing in your job and prioritize it. Then look at the items that have the highest priority—the ones that are the most fulfilling, meaningful, productive, and profitable.

Then take off the bottom 20 percent of that list, and give those tasks to somebody who would be inspired to do them. By using the time you've saving by taking those tasks off yourself, you can go out and produce more than the cost of that individual and they in turn can produce more return for you.

It's wise, and essential, to delegate in order to get yourself on to another level. Do that every quarter. Go to the list and see if there's any more responsibilities you can delegate, because you will not actualize your life as long as you're doing low priority or desperate things.

In the meantime, ask yourself about the actions that you're doing daily. If you're going to do them anyway, you might as well be inspired by them. Ask, "How is what I'm doing in my job helping me fulfill my highest values?" When you find that out, mundane jobs can then become inspiring.

Identify the 25 percent of tasks that give you the 75 percent of value, and keep doing those on a regular basis. Do this for everybody until they're all efficiently doing the tasks that most inspiring to them. Keep delegating things that are less inspiring so that all functions are being fulfilled by inspired people. And watch what a company will do. It can be amazing.

People come up to me and ask, "John, can you give me some ideas on how to stay focused and be more accountable? I've got all the hows, but I don't seem to do the things I believe are essential for me to do. Can you give me some tips?"

Absolutely. Again, when the why is big enough, the how will take care of itself. But you can do some things to help yourself become more accountable.

Simply begin identifying those highest priority action steps that you have done, or learned, that have proven to be most effective at achieving your highest values and purpose. I learned that from a great teacher named Ira Hayes, who carried around a highest priority checklist of all the things that he had proved to work in his life and read them every day. He increased the probability of doing those things just by having a checklist in front of him. I've been doing that for many years. I follow that checklist like clockwork. In the morning I review it, and I find that I get more out of my day.

Each day, when you discover something that works anywhere in your life, write it down on a master checklist. If you want to have a mastered life, create a master checklist every day. At the end of the day, go through that list and check off whether you acted upon or fulfilled those most important actions.

Make copies of this daily sheet and keep updating it, so you will have thousands of these sheets over the years. Then look for the highest priority of the highest priority of the highest priority actions in order to keep yourself ever more productive and inspired. As you go through the list, if for some reason you find out that you didn't do that item that day, concentrate on it tomorrow. If you find that you're still not doing it, consider giving yourself an incentive. Get yourself an accountability mentor or a coach, link it to your highest values, or practice the relevant skills to overcome any fear about doing this action or job.

The checklist is a self-accountability system. You cannot use it without raising your probabilities of achievement and self-worth. It helps you grow your confidence and your certainty, because when you do what you say you would, you grow and gain confidence.

A checklist is a simple process. I have thirty different things on my checklist that, if I do every single day, will help my life purpose to unfold. It just works. Every single morning, before you start the day, stop and reflect on your checklist. In the evening, check it off. Look for patterns; keep refining the list. Give yourself incentives—a coach, if necessary. If you find that something works, stick to it. Checklists keep you focused, and it is essential for you to be focused if you're going to live up to a great vision and create or attract great opportunities.

When you set goals that are not congruent with your highest values, you have resistance. But if you set goals in your business that are aligned to those values, you create assistance. Goals that are not congruent and even contradict other goals can become deleted by the brain. If you say, "I want to do this and this and this" and you add up all these items and find that they're contradictory or there's no time for them all, your brain can disregard or delete them all.

Set goals that align with your true higher values, and honor your unique form of business. Any time you think you're less "successful" than somebody else, you can begin to subordinate yourself to some other business leader's value systems. If you go against your own higher values, you'll discover and experience feedback mechanisms leading you back to what is more authentic. Like your body, your business will develop symptoms when you're not being true to yourself. These symptoms are just trying to get you to be true in yourself in the business.

Your relationship is giving you signs and symptoms to be true to yourself. Your social life is giving you feedback to be true to yourself. All areas of your life are trying to give you feedback to be true to yourself.

The world around you is a matrix trying to help us be authentic and love.

Once you determine exactly what your higher values are, create a strategy to fulfill them. If you don't know what they are, get a mentor to help you. Or sit down, brainstorm, and meditate. Sit there until you come up with a way. Or to be most efficient, simply log onto my website, DrDemartini.com, and you will find the Demartini Values Determination Process, which you can use to determine your values.

Stay focused on creating a strategy for fulfilling your mission and vision. Hold the vision and go inside. Don't stop until you get an insight on how to strategize it fully in your mind. Make a list of the things that you know work and the things you know don't work. You don't have to reinvent the wheel or relearn things, because if you follow a checklist, it will refine your skills. Create a checklist of what works every day. Write down what worked, keep a list, and read it. Keep doing what works.

Remember, the world treats you the way you treat yourself. If you value yourself, the world values you. Until you value yourself, don't expect others to. If you don't pay yourself first, don't expect anybody else to. You don't give yourself permission to do something great: why would the world give great opportunities to you? Simply allow yourself to be great and do something extraordinary. If you do, you'll be amazed what you can get out of yourself.

At one point when I was in my twenties, I called Linus Pauling, the two-time Nobel Prize winner, and he told me something that is with me for this day: "When I get up in the morning, one thing I dream about is going into the lab to see if I can't make one more contribution to humanity before I die." That stuck with me: to get up, go into the lab, and try to make one more contribution that can change the lives of human beings.

Sometimes we don't give ourselves permission to do something extraordinary. Instead we aggrandize other people, we minimize and disempower ourselves, and we hold ourselves back. We don't believe that we can stand on the shoulders of great people and do something greater.

Give yourself permission to do something meaningful and inspiring, but don't imagine something that's not really true or really aligned with your highest values; that's a fantasy. But with something that you know inside your soul you would love to do—declare it, go for it, and give yourself permission to do it. Tell yourself you are a genius, and you apply your wisdom. Watch what happens. I have had thousands of people start doing that and making an impact.

Next, have a mentor or a coach, because you will get more out of yourself if you do. I had a friend that had a $1.2 million company, but he realized he was not doing all the things that would help that company. So he decided to hire an elderly gentleman him $85,000 a year simply to make sure he did what he had on his agenda. His company went from $1.2 million to $10 million. Is it worth paying $85,000 to get $10 million? Absolutely. He had a coach. What would happen to a sports team if it didn't have a coach?

Once you have a coach, ask yourself, where's my originality? If you're authentic, you have something original inside you. Ask yourself, what is my unique mission and contribution and who actually am I? What is my original contribution to planet earth? If you are truly authentic, it's like a fingerprint of your own uniqueness. That's where your power is.

[3]

The Secret and Powerful Treasure of Wellness, Vitality, Beauty, and Fitness

Just as we have treasures in the mind, we have massive treasures in our body. What a great gift it is to have a great body to work with on a daily basis!

You may think, "I don't have such a great-looking body," but you can. It's all about perspective, and it's all about your actions. So let's discuss some of the treasures within your physical body, and let's look at how we can live a more purposeful and vibrant life physically.

Think about this for a second: if you have no meaningful reason to live, you may have a reason to die. The greater the reason, or meaningful purpose to live, the more you're going to get out of your body. In my experience, when somebody has some vitally important reason to do something with their body, vitality emerges automatically and spontaneously.

One time when I was in college, I was watching a man sitting on a couch, looking fatigued and frustrated. All of a sudden, a girlfriend called and asked if he could come by. In seconds, because he had something meaningful to pursue, he got up, cleaned, and shaved, and he was out of there. Seconds before, he'd been thinking, "I just want to sit around and not do anything," but the moment he had a high-value reason to get up and go, his vital energy soared.

I've watched this over and over again: when people have a great enough reason for being vital, they *are* vital. I've also sometimes found that people who have chronic fatigue are scattered and distracted, trying to live other people's lives, rather than being inspired intrinsically from within. They're trying to please everybody on the outside instead of listening to the internal voice and vision that could inspire them.

When you have a clear vision about what you want to do, a real powerful purpose, and a cause to get up and go, your body will automatically respond.

So one treasure you have inside you is pulling out of yourself a highest-value based reason for getting up and being vital. If you don't have a reason to live, you have a reason to die. If you don't have a reason for being vital, you have a reason to be fatigued. And if you try to live somebody else's life instead of your own, you're going to have scattered energies instead of focused power.

Dig inside yourself tonight. As you're about to go to sleep, ask what you would like to dedicate your life to. What inspires you? What do you love to do with your body? What inspiring objectives could you accomplish? You might want to have a piece of paper and a pen next to the bed so you can write these ideas down if they come into your mind.

In my experience, one of the most powerful things you can do for a long, vibrant life is to have something to live for. The great artists, who had the dream of painting when they were one hundred, lived for a long time. The great philosopher Giordano Bruno wrote a biography of what his life would be like five hundred years in the future so he would have something to live for every day.

I cannot overemphasize the significance of having a purpose, a cause, that fills your mind with goals. People who write down truly authentic, meaningful and inspiring goals get more out of their lives than people who don't. Those who have something to live for get much more out of life than people who don't.

Tonight, dream about what you want to live for. Look honestly at what your life demonstrates is truly most important to you. If ideas come to you in the night or morning, write them down. Create a story-board or vision book. Use the treasures of your mind to visualize and affirm your dream. Focus on it and write it down, because your mind affects your body, and having a goal keeps you more vitally alive.

Have a big dream; then the little things will take care of themselves. If your goal is to run a mile and you do it, you'll probably be sweating and tired at the end. But if your goal is to run ten miles, when you get to the one-mile mark, you're just warming up; you're not even sweating.

That's the way I would love for you to go. Allow yourself a big, vital life. Say to yourself, "I have incredible vitality; I have the power to live and do what I would love." In the process, you will vitalize your body.

If you have a big enough reason for doing something, you will find a way. If someone were to kidnap your family, you would find a way to get them back. When the why is big enough, the hows take care of themselves. The bigger your why, the bigger your life. If you want a vital body, find a why, a cause, a purpose, a mission—something to which you can dedicate your life for at least one hundred years, because you have the right to live at least one hundred years, and you have a body that can do it.

It's been proved that those who have a will to live are more likely to sustain their lives. I have observed people who have had strokes. Many times, they have either fulfilled all their goals and have nothing more to go for, or they've reached a point where they don't know how to fulfill the goals that still remain, and they feel futility; they see no light at the end of the tunnel. This is very common among people who have strokes.

Once I was on a ship. At the six o'clock social hour, a ninety-four-year-old woman came walking in, dressed beautifully, and asked, "Where's the party? Where's the action?" It's one of my dreams to be that playful at the age of ninety-four.

This lady had just flown in from Africa. At age ninety-four, she had just come down from climbing

Mount Kilimanjaro. She came in, asked where the party was at, and went around looking for young men to also take her to the theater. She came up to me and said, "Are you available?" So with two other gentlemen, I took this lovely lady to the theater onshore. We got out of the theater at 10:30 or 11:00 and came back to the ship. The lady was asking, "Where's the action? Where's the club? Which man is going to take me to the club?" I wasn't able to stay up with her, but she was still going at ninety-four years old. Talking to her the next couple of days, I found out that she had dreams, places to go, people to meet, and things to do.

I've mentioned Paul Bragg, who passed away at a ripe elderly age after doing many challenging feats, like swimming harnessed to a tugboat. This shows what's possible for a human being if your intention is clear and you're focused on your outcome: you can pull a tugboat. He has a daughter who is vital even into her eighties; she travels the world and still lectures, with a very intense schedule. She's still speaking, still writing books, still traveling the world. Is that alive?

If you have a will to live, you don't have a will to die; you have to something to do. The greater your cause, the greater your intention, the greater your willingness to do something, the greater chance you have of a longer life.

I encourage you to set goals not only in this life, but beyond this life. Most of the goals we set are only for this mortal body, because we think we are this mortal body. Why not assume we are immortal souls and set immortal goals and leave immortal legacies?

I want to share the next treasure that you have inside you. You probably know that your body weight consists of around 70 percent water. But it's a fact that the more water we have in our body, the more perfectly it functions. The joints are lubricated, the eyes work better, the mind thinks more clearly, the synapses in the brain are sharper.

When I'm talking about water, I'm not talking about tea, coffee, juices, or milk; I'm talking about water. It is not exactly the same as any other liquid. It is a universal solvent, which enables the body to function. The cells of your body and the little organelles inside them are surrounded by water molecules. When we have plenty of water molecules, the organs and enzymes function properly.

Furthermore, it's been found that if we're in a state of gratitude and love, the water molecules organize themselves into beautiful structures and allow the enzymes to do their dance. If we drink plenty of water, to the point where we actually can feel the fluids in our body—the coolness, refreshment, and vitality that water provides—our body is getting bathed. It's like taking a bath or going swimming, which is refreshing. We have a kind of tube that goes from the top to the bottom of the body. When we put water through ourselves on a daily basis, it cleanses, purifies, detoxifies, and tonifies our physiology.

Drink plenty of water. I know you've heard this before, but there is wisdom in being reminded to drink water daily. When I was in practice many years ago, I frequently found out that patients were literally dehydrated: much of the joint pains, muscle stiffness, and headaches were simply due to lack of water. Drink more water, and you'll see changes in your physiology, starting the next day. It's immediate.

We also require quality foods, because our diet has an effect on our physiology. You can see this if you do a self-analysis. I was introduced to this idea when I was about eighteen years old and came across the writings of Gandhi. He did a self-analysis about his diet. On a daily basis, he wrote down what he ate. He looked at how much he ate, how much fluid he drank, and he analyzed those relative to how he felt and how his mind thought. Then he wrote down the key things that he discovered about himself.

I thought, "If it's good enough for Gandhi, it's good enough for me." I started doing the same thing, and I did it for two years. I simply paid attention to what I ate and how I felt throughout the day. I learned more from that process than from any book I've ever read on diet. I found out, for example, that when I ate too many kinds of food, I tended to overeat. When I narrowed it down to smaller types of food, I didn't overeat as much. As a result, my vitality was greater, because eating too much food will sedate you. You tend to live longer if you eat moderately and even lightly, or occasionally fast. It's wiser to push yourself away from the table than to gorge yourself. It's not wise to live to eat, but it is wise to eat to live, and to live moderately that way.

Here are some things to do in your diet that you may not have thought about. Don't eat huge meals late at night, because I've seen that they frequently cause hiatal hernias and fatigue. Lying down, stuffed in the stomach, puts the diaphragm in an awkward position, and makes it difficult to breathe properly, so you lose your vitality. If you eat a huge meal, wait at least four hours before lying down. If you eat a moderate meal, wait at least three hours. If you eat a light meal, wait for two hours; if you eat a snack, maybe an hour. At any rate, don't eat and immediately lie down: it throws your digestion and metabolism off.

It's also been shown that your metabolism is at its peak in the morning and down in the evening. If you eat a little bit more in the morning than in the evening, you're probably going to lose weight, but if you eat late at night, you'll tend to gain weight. So again, it's wise not to eat heavy meals before you go to sleep at night.

It's also wise to eat food that has some degree of freshness and crispness. You don't want to eat limpy-wimpy, oily-boily, greasy-cheesy kinds of foods. You want fresh, quality food. It's worth the effort. You may think it costs a little bit more, but it actually costs less, because it adds more life to your life. Get quality food, get some raw and some cooked foods, and eat as many fresh natural foods as possible.

When you're eating, make sure that you're calm. If you are stressed when you're about to eat, it's wiser to stop, close your eyes, and think about what you're grateful for. If something's happened that you assume is not necessarily inspiring, ask how it helps you in your life, because everything has two sides and a corresponding advantage if you look carefully. Calm and center yourself, and meditate mindfully for a second. When you're distressed, your physiology makes your blood supply go to your muscles and bones rather than to the organs of digestion. If you're relaxed, you digest and absorb your food more efficiently, and you'll have greater vitality and less toxification.

When people say they have chronic fatigue syndrome, I tend to find that they have subordinated their dreams to somebody else's. They've injected other people's value systems into their lives; they're monitoring themselves and sacrificing themselves for those intentions that have been injected from without. They're going against their own highest values and will. It will drain any human being if they're not doing something that's truly meaningful and that inspires them. They're scattering themselves out into too many scattered areas, minimizing themselves for others, and failing to give themselves permission to be the magnificent people that they really are.

I also recommend that you mindfully meditate every day. If you want to have longevity, stop, meditate, calm yourself, and center yourself. Make a mental list of all the things you can be grateful for. When you receive an inspiring vision, write it down and concentrate your efforts and intention on it. Be receptive with your attention, and concentrate on your intention to create. Creation is part of our nature. If we don't create or we're not productive, we don't feel valuable, we don't feel alive, we don't feel our self-worth. But creativity with meaningful service will add years of vitality to our lives.

Also breathe deeply. A manic person will breathe with short exhalations and long inhalations. An individual that's depressed will do the opposite: short inhalations, with long exhalations. Long inhalations with short exhalations wake you up. Long exhalations with short inhalations sedate you.

Breathing, with an even balance between inhalations and exhalations, normalizes your physiology and brings about wellness. Long inhalation activates the sympathetic nervous system, and long exhalations activate the parasympathetic nervous system. Balanced breathing activates a synthesis: normal health, wellness, and longevity.

Until we can manage our emotions, we will not be able to as effectively manage our lives. We can equilibrate the mind by equilibrating the breath: it stabilizes and centers the mind, and the physiology responds accordingly.

Breathe in for seven seconds, hold it for seven seconds, breathe out for seven seconds, and again hold the breath for seven seconds. Train yourself to have balanced breathing, and watch your physiology return to balance.

Do you know that ungoverned extreme emotions become governed when you do this balanced breathing exercise? While you're doing it, you will calm down elation and uplift depression; balanced breathing normalizes and centers you.

If you take the elation and the depression and put them together, you synthesize them into love, because love is a synthesis of elation and depression, of attraction and repulsion; it's a synthesis of all complementary opposites, the synchronous balance of yin and yang.

In fact, if you look at the individual you're in a relationship with, you'll see that at times you're attracted, and at other times you're repelled. Sometimes you say to your partner, "Don't leave me," and a few moments later, you're saying, "Leave me alone. Get out of my sight." Love is the synthesis of attraction and repulsion.

If you practice these suggestions, you'll add vitality to your life. If you also have a clear vision of something to live for, you'll add even more vitality, and the treasures of your physiology will surface.

Use relaxation, balanced breathing, drinking water, meditation, and eating high quality food, combined with a long-range vision, and watch what happens to your physiology. It is waiting for you to have a dream and give it something to live for and to fuel it with quality food, water, and breath. When you do, your vitality will soar. Your physiology will allow you to accomplish the things that you deserve to, and you'll awaken the treasure of your body.

Imagine this: all the cells of your body know exactly what to do. You have trillions of cells, with trillions of biomolecules, working in every one of those cells. All of them are working harmoniously and in coordination. Imagine if we had to be responsible for figuring out every one of those biochemical actions and had coordinate them. There's an extraordinary hidden wisdom inside us. Even those that have won Nobel Prizes for biology are humbled before the intelligence of the body.

The treasure that's sitting there stored, waiting to come to the surface to bring health and well-being into our life, is enormous. Having been involved in the healing arts for decades, I've learned that your body is working for you, not against you.

In our society we have somehow gotten the idea that disease is bad. I want to share a different insight.

Sometimes signs and symptoms that we think are disease are actually feedback mechanisms to help us. My observations of thousands of people in clinical cases tell me that their bodies are often attempting to give them feedback.

Let me explain. Say you go out and have a pizza, and on top of that you drink a lot of orange juice, followed by a cheesecake, sauerkraut, and spare ribs. You keep going on, eating the most ungodly food combinations you can imagine.

When you wake up the next morning, you'll probably feel puffy and stuffy. You'll probably have indigestion, bloat, and gas. Now is that health or disease?

One approach is to say that is disease, and you need antacids and other remedies to cure these symptoms. But from my perspective, with all those symptoms your body is trying to give you feedback: "Hey, you're blowing it, you're eating too much, and you're not combining well." So maybe the body is trying to guide us to live more wisely and moderately, and according to priority.

From my observations working with people, particularly with mind-body relationships, the signs and symptoms of the body are forms of feedback to guide our mind and our actions back to poise and balance. In other words, if we encounter an event that we think is distressing, something we perceive to be more negative than positive, our physiology defends itself: it starts to take the blood supply out of the organs of digestion. We generate reactions that create what some label as disease, our immune system capacity goes down, and our physiology starts to weaken. If we continue to do that over a long period of time, we start to break down. But those reactions are giving us feedback to change our perceptions and look for opportunities to have a balanced perspective.

I had a gentleman come to me whose body was covered with psoriasis. It covered his joints, elbows, knees, and part of his face. He'd had it since he was a young child. He came to a signature program I present called *The Breakthrough Experience®*. He learned the *Demartini Method®*, which shows how to find the hidden order in the apparent chaos in life. When he was through, he had tears of gratitude towards a father from whom he had been alienated since he was a child. His father, he thought, was mean and violent to him. The man was initially angry. He had alienated himself from his father, and he'd been angry. From that day on, he started having psoriatic reactions.

When he finished the method I gave him, he saw the situation differently. Once he balanced his perspective, he found a way of loving his father. The depth of his most authentic self or soul wanted him to love his father, as all people do, and when he found that out, he had a catharsis, with tears in his eyes and sniffles in his nose. I gave him a hug afterwards, because he had such a great realization.

Later I got a letter from this gentleman. Within three days, some of the psoriasis scabs had started to calm, and within a week, they started to turn pink; in the next two weeks, they were totally gone. The psoriasis was a form of feedback to let him know that something in his life had not been completed and a subconsciously stored memory not balanced. He had an imbalanced perspective about his father, which was blocking him from feeling love and appreciation for somebody he cared for deeply. His physiology was trying to help him adjust that misperception.

The science of the mind-body is just emerging. In the decades to come, we will see more and more of it, and we'll start to learn exactly why our physiology does what it does. Illness is not just due to a virus or something similar; it occurs because somehow we have imbalanced our perspectives in our psyches. Our body is giving feedback to guide us and help us heal. This is something that I think the world deserves to know, and that's why I want to make sure you know you have that treasure inside you. If you meditate, listen to your intuition, and bring your perceptions back into balance, your body will let you know what is emotionally stored inside you that you haven't loved and appreciated, where you have an imbalanced perspective, and why you have distress.

You have the power to create the cells of your body; similarly, you have the power to heal and transform those cells. Love and gratitude are the greatest healers. Having certainty and presence in our life and love and gratitude in our heart is the key, and our body and mind are working together for this end.

When you have signs and symptoms of illness, maybe you will treat it from the conventional approach. But in the meantime, look deeper and discover what the ailment is guiding you to do. That way you're less likely to recreate it or generate another symptom to get you to complete that incomplete perception. If we have some distress that we don't dissolve or find out how it serves us, we automatically store it in our body in the form of signs and symptoms.

Dig deeper; find the treasure that's hidden in every event in your life. If you start to see distress, look again, and find the hidden order in there. Know that there's a way inside to the treasure, and that love and gratitude are the key that opens up the gateway of the heart, allowing that treasure to come to the surface. It is the key to healing, and your body is designed to be well. All that is required is to appreciate and love it and know that treasure.

I also recommend that you meditate and sit in silence on a daily basis, not just to be grateful but to visualize your body the way you want it. Nearly everybody has parts of the body they admire and dislike—even supermodels. One time I was consulting with a supermodel. Even though she looked fine to me, she did not appreciate half of her body.

I recommend that you go through all the things that you like and dislike about your body. Ask, how does the body, even the way it is, serve me? until you can be grateful for it. How do the parts of my body that I dislike serve me? Ask those questions, because your quality of life is based on quality of questions you ask. If you're not going to do something about these features, your mind can love them as they are. You want to find out exactly how your body serves you until you can say, "I am truly grateful to have the body that I have." If you are not appreciative of your body, it can break down. Appreciate what you've got; my mother taught me that when I was four years old.

Every time you perceive things, you evaluate them, and you project your values onto them. Sometimes you exaggerate or minimize them. Maybe you exaggerate the pleasure and minimize the pain, or vice versa. When you attend to something in your sensory world, you respond accordingly in your motor world. The motor world is not limited to your big muscles; it also includes the body's little microfilament muscles within your cells. They also respond to what you're perceiving.

When you have an imbalanced perception, you have both a conscious and unconscious awareness, some previous associations, and a reflex response. This response includes and affects the cells and muscles, causing muscular tensions and compressions. It also goes up into the brain, initiating emotional reactions in the form of seeking impulses and avoiding instincts, which then return and impose even more tensions and compressions on your cells and muscles.

Whenever you have an imbalanced perspective about the world around you, you see disorder, and you attract or repel, like or dislike, feel pleasure or pain; your cells become polarized. That creates tension and compression, which in turns causes too much or too little activity of the cell: this is what we call illness. Then the feedback from these cells goes back to the brain and lets it know that you're somehow distorting your reality. This distortion manifests in the form of symptoms. But actually the body is trying to let us know where we don't have a balanced perspective on life and where we're not loving and appreciating things. If we don't love and appreciate our body, it breaks down in order to humble us enough to appreciate and love it as it is. So when the body creates illness, it's actually giving us a gift: feedback on how to love our life, the people around us, and the parts inside us we haven't loved before.

Illness isn't bad. If we understand it and put it into context, it has also upsides, if it is wisely interpreted. Decoding your body's messages is the secret of the future of wellness care. In the decades to come, we'll able to discern the subtleties of what the body is saying so that we can change our perceptions and physiology in time to prevent illness from becoming extreme. This will be the future of the wellness industry in the years to come.

[4]

The Secret and Powerful Treasure of Love, Intimacy, Caring Communication, and Family Dynamics

Our family and our relationships are a treasure chest that we are wise to appreciate and love. If we stop and think about it, interaction with other people is one of the greatest feedback systems to authenticity we have.

I'd like to share some of the keys to opening up the treasure of relationships. Maybe they relate to your family, or if you're not married yet, to special people in your life.

In our lives, we have a unique set of values, as does everyone we interact with, and we all function from the perspective of those values. The highest priority of your values dictates how you sense and act on the world. If we're going to communicate with others, we are wise to truly come to know them. Consequently, knowing our values and those of the people we love is important if we're ever going to communicate effectively and have meaningful relationships.

I'd like to share with you one of the first relationship treasures: the treasure of knowing your own individual values, as well as those of others. Here are thirteen determinants.

1. How do people most commonly fill their intimate and personal space? If you look at somebody's office cubicle, you'll see certain things: pictures of their kids; trophies, if they're into sports; pictures

of places they've been to, if they're into traveling. How they commonly fill their intimate and personal space tells you a lot about what's important to them, and you will probably not communicate respectfully with people unless you know what's important to them.

2. How do they spend their time most? Everybody has enough time for things that are really important to them and they seldom if ever have enough time for things that aren't.

3. How do they spend their energy most? If somebody comes up to you and offers you an opportunity to do something that's really important to you, you'll muster up the energy, and you'll get moving. But if somebody comes up to you and says they're going to do something that has no meaning or value to you, you'll say, "Look, I'm a little tired. I'd like to take it easy tonight."

4. How do they spend their money most? People find a way to have enough money for things that are really important to them, but they don't want to spend on things that aren't. In a relationship, the husband wants to buy things that are important to him, and the wife wants to buy things that are important to her. She thinks what he is spending money on is not important, and he thinks what she's spending money on is not important. Both of them are projecting their values onto the other

partner and assuming that they're spending money unwisely, but the reality is that people spend their money according to their highest values.

5. Where are you most organized and ordered? You bring organization and order to what you value most.

6. Where are you most focused, reliable, and disciplined? Whatever is highest on your list of values you spontaneously do consistently without needing reminding or external motivation.

7. What do they think about most—about how they would love their life to be—that shows evidence of coming true? Your innermost dominant thought creates your outermost tangible reality. And what people think about most reflects their highest values. In other words, if you have idle time, your mind automatically goes to the things that you value most. That's what it focuses on, and you will think and dream accordingly. Do you want to know how people think and what they think about? If you have a conversation with them, they'll bring it around to where they can talk about what's important to them.

8. What do they visualize and dream about—about how they would love their life to be—that shows evidence of coming true? If you ask someone, what's your dream in life? they'll focus on what's important to their lives. They key is to identify

what they are visualizing that is actually coming true not just their fleeting fantasies or disturbing distractions.

9. What do they talk to themselves about most—about how they would love their life to be that shows evidence of coming true? They are frequently talking to themselves about their dream, what's important to them. To find this out, you may simply ask them or maybe listen to their own conversations with themselves.

10. What do they converse about most with other people? What is their more common external dialogue? At a social function, everybody will, again, bring the conversation over to what is important to them. If you start talking about things that are important to them, they'll liven up, they'll want to get involved, and they'll think they're having a great time. If you start talking about things that aren't important to them, they'll shut down, withdraw, walk away, or even go to sleep.

11. What inspires them and what do they emotionally react to? If you say something to them and they smile, you're obviously supporting their values. If they frown and withdraw from you, you're obviously going against their values. Pay close attention to those responses, because they tell you the person's values and how they react emotionally.

Whatever is highest on their list of values will inspire them and even bring tears of gratitude to their eyes as a confirmation of a moment of their authenticity.

12. What goals are they most consistently and persistently pursuing and achieving? If you ask somebody to write down the ten most important things they want to accomplish in life, I guarantee you, they will focus on the things that are important. In the areas that are not important to them, they won't even know where to begin. Goals reflect values.

13. What do they most love to learn about, study, read about, or watch on YouTube? Everyone loves to spontaneously learn about what is truly most important to them—their highest value.

The first thing you want to do if you want to have a relationship with anybody is (1) know your hierarchy of values and (2) get to know theirs, because if you can't communicate your highest values, or what is most important to you in terms of theirs, you've got no relationship. The number one secret of relationships is the art of communicating your highest values in terms of their highest values. How is anybody going to value you if you can't communicate in terms of their most meaningful values? Your and their most authentic identities revolve around both of your highest values.

As we've seen, every individual has a hierarchy of values: the thing that is most important to them, the second most important, the third most important, and so on. They derive those values from what they most perceive as missing. If you perceive yourself as lacking a relationship, you look for relationship. If you perceive yourself as lacking money, you look for money. If you perceive that you're not having clients or business, you look for business. Whatever is perceived as most missing becomes most valuable. In fact, the word *fulfillment* means filling the mind with what is perceiving as missing or empty. *Satisfaction* means the situation of fulfillment.

These values drive the human being. If anything comes along to support your value system, you call it good, and if it goes against your value system, you call it bad.

Our morals and ethics are based on these value systems, which also dictate our destiny. The hierarchy of your values dictates how you see the world and attend to the world as well as how you intend and act upon the world.

Let me give you an example. Say a husband and wife are walking in a mall. The wife's highest values may center on the children, and the husband's highest values are possibly business, finance, intellectual stimulation, and computers. As they're walking the mall, holding hands, they see a little store with children's clothes and health items. The woman will automatically say, "Oh, honey! Let's stop in here for a second." She'll start to get attention surplus order, and he'll get attention deficit disorder.

As they walk further down the mall, if they see a computer store, bookstore, or something that would help the man build his business, he'll wake up, he'll have attention surplus order, and she'll get attention deficit disorder. She will start yawning and say, "I'll meet you outside in thirty minutes."

Because the wife's highest value is children, she will see opportunities for children that he won't see, and he will see opportunities for businesses that she won't. Consequently, the opportunities in an individual's life have everything to do with their hierarchy of values.

I was walking in the mall one day, and saw a gentleman I know who's really a successful entrepreneur; he's very sharp in business and has a lot of businesses. That's his highest value. My highest value is studying the laws of the universe as they relate to human behavior.

As we walked, we came across a bookstore. I wanted to go in. The gentleman noticed opportunities to sell products and businesses. As he was walking, he was saying, "There's a great business, look at it, look at all the people buying. There must be a big run on that. I can start a new business and make a fortune, or possibly invest in that company."

He's thinking of business; I'm thinking of books. I'm not seeing business opportunities; he's not seeing books. In short, we filter and act upon the world according to our current (but ever evolving) hierarchy of values, which dictates our destinies, and the series of our destinies determines our life journey.

Next I would like to discuss the key to matching and communicating your values to those of the other individual. Think about this: say the wife's highest values are her family, and her husband's highest values have to do with his business. This is not uncommon: about 75 percent of people live this way. If he is talking to her about his business, projecting his higher values onto her, and expecting her to be that way, he's going to alienate her, and she's not going to feel loved or cared for. She's going to feel unappreciated or minimized. If she does the same, expecting him to live according to her higher values, that too erodes the relationship. It's not necessary for two people to have exactly the same values in a relationship—that's what makes us unique—but we do want to honor the other individual's values.

Here's a little key to opening up the treasure of value communication in your life. Identify what your highest values are, what your life really demonstrates—not fantasies, not what you think it should be, not what society expects, but what truly is. Do the same thing for the other individual, whether it's your spouse, one of your children, someone at work, or a client. Determine the values of those individuals; unless you do, you will struggle to communicate your own goals or dreams to them.

By following the thirteen determinants that I listed above, or by visiting drdemartini.com and filling in the Demartini Value Determination Process on line and then taking the top two or three of your highest values, and the top two or three of your partner's demonstrated highest values you can begin to more effectively and respectfully communicate. Ask the simple question: how does them fulfilling their highest three values help me fulfill mine? And how does my highest three values help them fulfill theirs?

At first, you're going to hit a roadblock and think, "I don't know how they do." That's why your wanting to change them, or fix them, or make them be different. But the mastery of life is the willingness to look deeper beyond first appearances. Learn to communicate what you think is important in terms of their highest values and what they think is most important.

Ask the question again: how is what they dedicate their life to and what's most important to them going to help you fulfill what you would love, what is most important to you?

For example, let's take the case above: the wife's highest values involve her family, and the husband's involve the business. He can stop and say, "How is her dedicating her life to raising a family helping my business?"

At first, he may think, "I don't know. It's time-consuming. It costs money." But he's wise to look at it differently. How does he do it? Having a family demonstrates success. It helps him in his business image. It also sets an elevated standard for them. She is great at raising the standard, making sure the home is beautiful, the kids are dressed nicely, they have a great education, and they have greater wellness. That reflection of him helps him in his business.

Ask, "How is what's important to the other individual serving me?" If you can't see it, you're going to spend your life trying to change the other individual, which will erode and possibly destroy the relationship. Then turn around and ask, "How is my dedicating my life to business helping her accomplish her goals with our family?"

The wife can see that her husband's spending time at work is providing an income, it's helping children go to a higher-quality school, and things of this nature.

Come up with at least ten, fifteen, twenty, twenty-five or even thirty links. The more links that you can make between what is important to you and what is important to the other individual, the more respectful and meaningful communication you have in that relationship. Everybody wants to be appreciated for who they are according to their own higher values. They don't want to be shouted at, they don't want to be told they have to, they want to be loved for who they are. The only way to do that is to find out what's important to them and honor that by finding out how it serves you, and vice versa. No great treasure can come out of a relationship unless there's an art of love and communication.

If you project your values onto the other individual, you are being careless, because you care less about their values than yours. If you minimize yours and exaggerate what's important to them, you're sacrificing your life, which builds resentment over time.

But if you learn the art of communicating, linking what's important to you to what's important to them and communicating your values in terms of theirs, magic occurs, because caring is crucial in a marriage, or any enduring relationship.

Make sure that you're communicating your highest values in terms of the other individual's without sacrificing or minimizing either theirs or your own. Take the time to determine their highest values. We may think we don't want to take that time, but in fact it saves us enormous amount of time in arguments, frustrations, aggravations, and doubts. Take the time to determine the other individual's values, link your values to theirs, and watch the treasure of caring communication emerge.

Most people are in relationship with fantasy figures, expecting them to be somebody they're not. Here's a sign that you've got a fantasy: you say things like, "They've got a lot of potential." Whenever you say that, it means you're projecting your values on them, and you're going to punish them if they don't measure up and you probably have an unrealistic expectation of who they are supposed to become.

Now here's the funny thing about relationships: you have a guessing game. Because you see the world a certain way, you may assume that everybody else does. You don't tell the other individual what your expectation is; they're supposed to guess. You expect them to read your mind and punish them when they don't. When they do, you say, "Oh, you're finally doing what I expect."

You've probably had the thought of marriage running around in your mind since childhood. Fairy tales have left us with images of Cinderella and Prince Charming or something similar, and we sometimes set up ourselves for fantasies and unrealistic expectations. We spend our lives comparing the men and women in our relationships to these fantasies, which can result in what seem to be devastation and setbacks.

I'd like to take a little reality check about relationships. We won't find the real treasure in a marriage if we keep comparing our spouse to fantasies. It will unfold, unveil itself, and glimmer only if we get down to the real truth, which is greater than the fantasies; even though we think the fantasies are going to be more fulfilling, they're not.

If we look carefully, we'll discover something new about ourselves in the process. As we've seen, you go through your life with a set of values, and you strive for whatever is highest on that scale. Lo and behold, you fall into a relationship with somebody who seems to have a different or even the complementary opposite set of values.

You think you want somebody totally like you, so they'll agree with you and do things that you want to do, but nature doesn't work that way. Nature makes sure that the areas that are *not* your highest values are filled with people that have them as theirs. Although we keep looking for things that support us, we keep getting things that both support and challenge.

In other words, the things that are lower on our value scale are typically filled in by somebody else who has them higher on theirs. About 75 percent of men focus on intellectual pursuits and business and financial development, and about 75 percent of women focus on relationships, social lives, health, and beauty. That doesn't mean that as a female, you can't focus on the other areas, because 25 percent of females do. But often that 25 percent attracts men who reflect their disowned parts and focus on the other side: social and physical relationships.

In short, whatever is lower on our value scale typically shows up in our relationships. This is quite humorous, because we assume we're looking for somebody that's going to bring us happiness, while in actuality, they bring us a loving balance of support and challenge. They make us dig into ourselves and own things that we may not have wanted to own or face and help make us whole and more authentic.

That's really where growth begins. The purpose of marriage, in my opinion, is growth—growth in the willingness to embrace our whole self, to take even the things that aren't initially important to us, discover how they serve us, and hold them dear to our heart.

I often say that I'm not even looking for happiness in relationships, although that's probably going to shock some people. In fact, I have a new book that's someday going to come out called *I Gave Up Happiness: It Made Me Too Sad.* I keep finding people that are setting up themselves for something to support their values alone. They keep seeking, and they don't want any challenge in life. But we also require somebody that challenges us, and maybe challenges are the things that make us grow.

A wise and fulfilling relationship is thus going to have a balance of support and challenge, moments of happiness and sadness, moments of being nice and mean, and even sometimes kind and cruel. That's what makes us grow.

I want us to have, not fantasies of happily ever after, but realities, knowing that when somebody challenges us, it's helping us grow. If you look carefully in the relationship, you'll see that your partner may not focus on the thing that you think is so important. You try to project your values onto them, but they're just not going to relate.

This teaches us to care about another individual in terms of their scale of values, which are usually the things that are lower on ours. That way, we get to embrace all of our values, become more well-rounded, and have fullness in life. Happiness is half-fulfillment, sadness is the other half of fulfillment, and true love is fulfillment, embracing the whole of our life and the other individual with us.

When you get into a relationship, if you think it's supposed to be happy, nice, and peaceful all the time, you set yourself up for fantasy and addiction. It's like a magnet: if you chop it in half trying to get only the positive side, you won't succeed: you'll always get a positive and negative. If you go into relationship looking for one side, a positive only, without allowing and embracing the other aspects, you're going to miss out on the magnificent love that surrounds you. True love has both sides—a balance of support and challenge, times of niceness and meanness, kindness and coolness.

If that idea challenges you, look honestly into your relationships. The individual you love—maybe your child—will at times do things that you perceive to be supportive to your highest values and at other times will do things that you perceive to be challenging. Conversely, if you look at how they see you, you find that you're perceived to be both supportive and challenging to them.

True love honors both sides. How are you going to have the magnetism you want in your life if you're not willing to embrace both sides of the magnet? True marriage is a balanced magnetism. That's why in relationships we attract our disowned parts: to help us own our full self so we can live fully. Marriage is designed to help us grow in love and fulfillment, not to pursue unsustainable fantasies. Each of us have two sides. And we would love to be loved for both sides. Fulfillment honors both.

Determine your values, then determine the values of the people that are close to you—your loved ones, your mate, your kids, people at work, customers, whoever—know their hierarchy of values. How are you going to have a meaningful and loving relationship if you can't communicate your values in terms of theirs and can't understand and appreciate their supportive and challenging sides?

Once a doctor from Ohio came to one of my Breakthrough Experience workshops. Later he called me and said, "Dr. Demartini, I am sending my wife to meet you in New York."

"What's the primary objective?"

"She needs fixing."

"Can you come along?"

"No, she's coming alone."

The guy paid me thousands of dollars to spend the day with his wife. I went to the hotel where she was staying, sat down with her, and said, "Your husband says you two have been having some challenges."

"Yeah, we've been having a lot of fights lately, and he thought that you'd be able to help me with my concerns and expectations."

"The first question I would love to ask you is, what is most important to you? What is highest on your list of values?"

We went through my value determination process and determined her values, and it was a pretty classic case. Her kids were most important, her house was important, her family was important, beauty, health for the kids—the classic traditional things.

"What are your husband's highest values?" I asked.

"Work, making money, golf, fancy cars, socializing, and smoking cigars." She had his values pretty well laid out.

"If you ranked them by priority, what's the highest priority for him?

"Business."

"What's your highest priority?"

"My family."

"How is his building his business helping you with the family?"

"It's not; it's interfering with the family. He's never home."

"So how is your spending time with the kids helping his business?"

"I don't know."

If she can't see how what's most important to her is helping him, and he can't see what's most important to him is helping her, there's a rocky relationship.

There's a beautiful principle in quantum physics called *entanglement*. It says that from the primordial soup of the universe, a singularity gave rise to all manifestation; therefore everything is ultimately connected in some form. Using that realization, I thought, "Everybody's value system on the planet is aiding and equilibrating somebody else's."

Somebody in the world has a value system opposite to yours. Can you picture that? Comically, you often find that person and marry them.

Marriage is not designed for hedonistic happiness—except in moments. The only people who buy that are gullible and a bit immature. Its purpose is not for happiness; its purpose of meaningful marriage is to equilibrate you and to help you be authentic. If you're cocky and self-righteous and exaggerate yourself, your partner's job is to deflate you, humble you, and bring you back to center, so your heart can open. At the same time, if you come home feeling down and deflated, what does your partner do? They let you know that you're not all that bad. They lift you up, don't they?

If somebody comes up to you and puts you down and you go lower, they want to lift you back up. Somebody tells you, "You're just a rotten scum of the earth."

You say, "You're right, I don't deserve to live. Shoot me; get it over with."

If you go down lower than they want to put you, they'll lift you back up, saying, "Maybe I'm overreacting; you know, come on."

But say somebody comes up and says, "Dr. Demartini, that was a great job. You're wonderful, man; you're the greatest."

If I go higher, saying, "Imagine how long it took you to figure that out," they'll slam me again.

When you go higher than people want to put you, they'll pull you down. When you go lower, they'll lift you up. It's human nature.

If I don't know how to communicate in terms of other people's highest values and go around self-righteously projecting my values onto them, what I have is carelessness. I'm exaggerating me and minimizing them. If I do the opposite, minimizing myself and putting them up on a pedestal, I'm being careful; I'm walking on eggshells. But when I neither put the other individual up nor put them down, but put them in my heart, I have caring. This is what keeps rings on fingers.

When I was consulting with this lady, we identified her values and her husband's values; then I spent the day linking them, asking, "How does your highest value help him get his highest values? And how does his highest value help you get what you want?"

We went back and forth until we came up with about 250 to 300 links (because they're there; everything in the universe is linked). We asked how his work was helping her. He was making the money, so they had a nicer home, better education, nicer clothes, higher social status, and a better self-image.

Then we asked her how her work at home helped her husband. "I have social parties at our beautiful home," she replied. "It makes him look more stable and successful, so more people want to do business with him, making him more money."

When I got through, she appreciated him for who he was instead of who he was supposed to be. When you finally appreciate and love people as they are, they turn into whom you love. Otherwise, you're having an affair with a fantasy figure, expecting them to live against their higher values, which is futile.

I went on to train the wife, like in a sales training program. I trained her about how to communicate within his highest values.

When she got home, she went to a sporting goods store. She bought a magazine on golf, three golf balls, and a golf shirt.

When he came back, she said, "I was on the way home, and I was thinking about you. I stopped off and bought you some golf balls. Are these the ones you like to use? And would you wear this shirt? I'll be glad to go back and get another one.

"I was reading this magazine about golf," she went on. "It's really interesting. I noticed that the tournament you go to every year is coming up. I'm always bitching at you for going, because it's always on the weekend when I want to do something with the kids.

"I called Momma, and I found out that there's a white sale on that weekend. I could go over to go where Momma is and take the kids there. They can see Grandma, we can go to the sale, and the amount I can save will pay for the entire trip. We need these things anyway. I could go there and save you money."

At the end, he said, "Maybe it's best to take the credit card."

Shortly after that, I got a letter from him. It said, "What a difference in our relationship! Thank you for what you did." He did not know that I'd spent the entire day with his wife, teaching her how to get whatever she wanted from him, and he paid me for it.

Many times in my seminars, I have people come up to me and say, "You know, Dr. Demartini, my mother abandoned me when I was four," or "My father died when I was six," or "We had a divorce in our family," or "My brother passed away young." Many times people focus on what they think they're missing.

What I am about to say here may challenge you at first. But I want you to think deeply, beyond your normal thinking, because I guarantee there's great gift and a great treasure in this one.

Nothing is missing. I have experienced this with my own life and family and received feedback from thousands of my students and clients. When you really look, you'll see that when somebody leaves your life, either through death or departure, there is not really abandonment; there is transformation. The masters of life understand transformation, but the ordinary individual lives in illusions of gain and loss and often victim labels. They're hoping someday to gain something that they think they don't have, but which in truth they do. And they think that they've lost something, when in actuality, they haven't.

When you think you've lost something from somebody or somebody wasn't there for you, I want you to write down the traits you think are now missing. You will discover that the traits you think you're missing are the ones that you admired and were infatuated with; they won't be the ones that you disliked and resented. You will not miss the things you resent; you will only miss what you're infatuated with. That means instead of seeing the individual in wholeness, you actually had an infatuation with parts of them and put them on a pedestal. That's why it hurts when they leave.

In actuality, nobody's worth putting either on pedestals or in pits, but they are all worth putting in the heart. If we look carefully at what we think is missing and break down the traits that appear to be suddenly gone—the way they hugged us, the way they looked at us, the way they talked to us—we can ask, who now has emerged in our lives to bring those things into our life? If we look carefully and don't stop until we see it, we'll discover it's there every time.

Let me give an example, I was working with a gentleman in South Africa whose son was killed. I asked him, "What did you miss most when he passed away?"

"Putting on his shoes, and playing ball with him, and doing things of this nature."

"So when he passed away, who emerged in your life to start to do those things?

"I don't know. Nobody showed up."

"Look again," I said.

His wife, who was sitting there said, "Oh, my God. You said that? When our son passed away, the next day you went out and bought tennis shoes—you've never worn tennis shoes since I have known you—and you started picking up sports. You started to take on some of the traits that he had. It's almost like you're carrying him around in you now."

This is what I've observed. When somebody leaves our life, somebody else brings into our life that which they represented. Identify those traits and ask, who is now bringing them, and what are the benefits of these new traits? And what were some of the drawbacks of the previous individual who has passed on so as to break the lingering infatuation.

You will discover that really nothing is missing. It's just changed form. Then you will feel the new form while honoring the presence of the individual who has departed. It's empowering to do this instead of wallowing in remorse, bereavement, and grief, which are blocks to love. They are merely the remnants of an addiction to things we were infatuated with. People deserve love, not infatuation. This realization frees us to feel the loved one's presence and move on with our lives. Otherwise we're holding on to the past instead of being present and going on to the future with our dreams. Nothing is missing; it's just in a new form. The second we realize this, we will open up the treasures inside our lives instead of living in pain and loss.

In your relationships, I would love for you to realize that you have a mother, a father, a sister, a brother, a spouse, a friend, even a grandparent and grandchild, all the time in your life. They're just changing forms. A child who loses a mother and father will take a doll and convert it into a mother and father. She will have the doll talk to them and scold them like a mother and father. Or she'll turn around and act like the mother and father to the doll to complete the family dynamic. This demonstrates that nothing is missing. Or possibly an aunt, or grandmother, or older sister will suddenly emerge and play the mother's role.

Instead of acting like a victim, thinking you're missing something, gain victory. Open up the treasure chest inside your awareness by asking quality questions, and you'll discover that there's nothing missing in your life. When you do, you'll come from a state of empowerment and fulfillment. Then the treasure chest is open, and all of a sudden you've got diamonds; you can shine; you can allow your life to be full.

In a relationship, realize that no matter what you do, you're going to be both praised and reprimanded. If you grow cocky, they'll nail you. If you grow too humble, they'll lift you.

Your kids are, by the way, are genetic expressions of your repressions. With every single thing that you disown and repress in your life, you activate a gene that manifests and pushes your buttons. If you ever expect full-time peace in the family, you are living in a fantasy. It's not designed to be only peaceful. Every family dynamic is designed to have both peace and war, calm and turmoil. At times you cooperate; at times you compete. When the mother and father are fighting, the kids are joined together. When the mother and father are at peace, the kids are fighting.

When one of the children is getting along with the father, the mother or sibling gets angry with the same child. The child says, "Mom's weird today."

The father says, "Oh, don't worry about it. She's just in that period of the month."

At another time, mommy's getting along with one of the children, and the father is not. The mother says, "Don't pay attention to it; he's got a business problem." Peace and war are both present.

Any time you expect peace, you're going have to have neighbors that are at war with you. Comically, the way to have a peaceful family is to be collectively at war with the neighbors.

The great discovery is that at any time in your life, when somebody is praising you, recommending you, being nice to you, someone else is being mean to you. Expecting one side without the other is like trying to have a one-sided magnet. Life is like a magnet. It's futile to try to get one side without the other, but if you embrace both sides, you realize that you've got a gift. Most people going around saying, "I'm not perfect yet." What if they are, and you're just expecting them to be one-sided?

There's a time when you realize that when you're nice to somebody, somebody else is mean to them. When you're mean to somebody, someone else is nice to them. When somebody is mean to you, someone else is nice to you. When someone is nice to you, somebody else is mean to you. If everybody's nice and supportive to you, if you don't have somebody to beat you up, you beat yourself up. It's all balancing; both sides are needed in the matrix—all to balance us and make or keep us authentic.

I'd rather be beaten up by somebody else, because then at least it's part-time, than beat myself up full-time. People that oversupport can you make you dependent; people that challenge you can make you independent. In the world, there are entrepreneurs and intrapreneurs. The people who perceived they have been challenged often become the entrepreneurs; the people who perceive they have not been challenged often become the intrapreneurs, working for other people, looking for a place to plug in the umbilical cord. You want to empower all seven areas of your life.

If you look carefully within, you will find you have every trait—you've got them all. We're like holographic people. You won't get rid of a trait. Have you ever tried to get rid of a trait in somebody else, say in your spouse? It's futile. It's not going to work. It doesn't work. It has not worked for thousands of years, yet we are still trying.

You can't even change yourself. You think, "I'm going to be only positive today." Then some weird, funky thing shows up that makes you angry and negative. Have you noticed that? You're not designed merely to be positive. You're designed to be balanced.

I've got every trait. I'm nice, I'm mean, I'm kind, I'm cruel, I'm giving, I'm taking, I'm generous, I'm stingy, I'm honest, I'm deceptive. It is wise to reflect and see the truth of and honor my whole nature.

No matter what anybody says about you, it's true. If you can own it and see how it serves you, it will just roll off your back; it won't affect you. It's only when you don't own the things people say about you that your button is pushed. It makes you angry; it makes you react. No matter what they say, you've got every trait; just own it, and realize they've got every trait too. Don't ever expect people to lose or gain traits. They're eternal; people are born with them, just like all other traits. They are all needed at various moments in our lives, where they greatly serve. The more you try to repress any of them, they more they become expressed.

[5]

The Secret and Powerful Treasure of Social Influence, Leadership, and Legacy

The next treasure that we're about to unveil is the power of our social treasure. Years ago, I made a list of people I would love to meet in my life—great celebrities, great leaders, great people that have left or are leaving a mark on history. I wrote them down, because I'm a firm believer that what you write down, look at, think about, visualize, and affirm, you manifest.

Some of the names I wrote down these names were film celebrities; others were great leaders; still others were Nobel Prize winners. At that time, it seemed like a far stretch, because I thought, "How am I going to meet these people?"

Somehow I found myself either in the right restaurant or in a plane sitting next to them. It was serendipitous.

I believe that our innermost dominant thought becomes our outermost tangible reality. If we have a vision of meeting great people, we will attract the people, places, things, ideas, events, and synchronicities that allow us to meet them.

You might ask, "Why would he want to meet these people?" My experience is that if you start to associate out with people that have an impact in the world, it brings out of you what you're capable of. You're capable of doing the same; it doesn't really matter what or where you started from.

When I was a teenager, I lived on the streets. I used to panhandle. Sometimes I went into restaurants, looking around for leftover food on the tables. I know what it's like to have nothing, but I also know what it's like to live in penthouses and on a giant yacht and associate with global leaders. The difference between where I was and where I am now is simply that I had the courage to acknowledge that I could resonate with leading influencers and that there is nothing less than or missing in me. In case you haven't already, I want you to right now to give yourself permission to associate with anybody that you'd love to meet.

I had it as a goal to meet John F. Kennedy Jr., who has the same birthday that I have (November 25). Later I had the opportunity to live a few doors down from him in New York City's Upper East Side and walk and converse with him and actress Daryl Hannah. It wasn't exactly how I initially envisioned it, but I attracted the people, places, things, ideas and events to make it happen, because I'd written it down, visualized it, and affirmed it, and I was willing to take an action step toward it. I believe that when an individual believes they have something global to offer in life, somehow it can stick with you. It can open up the possibility for you to bring it out.

Some psychologists and neurologists don't believe in the existence of the soul, the state of unconditional love, or the authentic self, but I believe that we have an inspired part of us that yearns inside to make a difference and to do something great or grand that could potentially leave an immortal legacy. Although our fears and guilt hold us back, our soul calls us to ever greater spheres and greater heights. If we listen to that immortal soul inside us, we can do something amazing in the world—not small things, but global things. If we open our hearts and minds to that possibility, make a list of the people that are doing those things, and believe that we have every trait we see in them, we will resonate with those individuals and uplevel our playing field. We will attract the people, places, and things to make those meetings happen.

Make a list of the people you'd love to meet; then go in and find out where you have all their admired traits in yourself (don't give up until you see them, because you do have them). Read your list and visualize it. Take some action steps if you feel enough courage. And blow your mind on the possibilities of whom you can meet and the opportunities that might open up, enabling you to play on a global level. Even if you're in a small town and you're doing a simple job, make a list of how that job touches the world through the ripple effect. Think of how that product, service, or idea touches others, gives them opportunities, and spreads across the world.

Allow yourself to believe you are worthy of global functioning. Watch what happens in your imagination if you focus on these things, because you deserve to be somebody who makes an ever greater difference.

The next thing is whom you associate with. If you associate with people that are thinking small, they want to keep you smaller; if you associate with people who think bigger, they will help you play bigger. Hang out with people that are stretching you. Keep asking, who can help me stretch? Who pulls more out of me than I generally pull out of myself?

When I met Paul Bragg, I was living with a group of guys in a tent. Later, I found out what happened to some of the other guys that lived there. One of them died of cocaine addiction. Another is in an old folks' retirement village because he OD'd on drugs and has psychiatric issues. Another is homeless. This is no joke. If hadn't met Paul Bragg, I probably would not even be alive today.

The people you associate with make a difference. If you want to be a leader, hang out with people who are leaders. You will expand yourself. But in turn it is wise and meaningful to encourage other people to give themselves permission to do the same. If I am now blessed to live an amazing life, it is time for me to pass the torch and help other people give themselves permission to do the same thing. If I can start out on the streets and then go on to have the things that I have today, I guarantee that somebody else can do the same.

It would be inspiring to me, when I'm about seventy or eighty years old, to take some time to go around in the streets, having nothing—just to know, when I have so much, what it's like to have so little again. And when I'm ninety old, if I'm still alive, I'm going to find a seventeen-year-old and pass on the torch. Those are two things that I'd love to do.

So why not go for it? Give yourself permission to do something outrageous. Give yourself permission to live an amazing life. You deserve it. Ask, where do you want to play in the game of life? What level of society do you want to play on?

When you start out as a child, your parents set the rules. When you're around eighteen, you defy your parents; you start thinking independently. Now the people who set the rules are social peers, people at work and people at school.

Then you finish school. Maybe you start your own business instead of working for somebody else; now you're setting the rules yourself. Your teachers and parents no longer have power over you, and you've already transcended some of your friends. Now you have some degree of power. But now the city rules are overpowering you. Eventually you grow a company citywide, and you become friends with the people in city politics. Now those people no longer rule you, because you know their game, and you're participating in it.

Then, as your company continues to grow, you come up against state rules; the state government now rules you. Eventually you have a multi-state company and start to have influence across the state. The state doesn't want to lose you, because you employ lots of people. You have influence in the state, but you now you face the rule of the national government. You eventually develop a multinational corporation, and you have influence across various nations. If one nation is upset with you, you can just close down and open up in another nation. You have a global effect, you are multinational, so the national governments don't rule you. But now world governments and organizations rule you.

Finally you get beyond that level. You are the sage, you see beyond all those things, and now you are ruled by universal laws. The people at the top are the ones that are most free. They can see the vision. The people at the bottom have all the pressure on them.

At or closer to the top is where I wanted to play in the game of life. If I am hanging out with people at the bottom, I am likely to be subordinate to others' values and live under perceived authority. I'm not automatically as seemingly free to actualize my life's dreams. But if I continually empower myself and grow by loving people and loving myself enough to honor my vision, and if I keep expanding my mind, educating and empowering myself in all areas, I will eventually rise to create or contribute to the next collective social value system.

Einstein said, "To punish me for my contempt of authority, Fate has made me an authority myself." His unwillingness to submit to perceived authority, looking instead at the laws of the universe, is what made him a superauthority who is immortal today.

That's what you can do in your leadership. You can allow yourself to receive, to serve, to climb and rise, because it's your nature to do so. As I've said, nobody gets up in the morning and says, "I want to be less powerful; I want to be subordinate."

Take a society that disempowers itself with dictators. We applaud for them when they break through and regain a free nation. The same thing occurs in our life. We deserve to live a free life, which is when you can really say, "I do what I love, I love what I do. I love the people I am doing it with, and I love sharing my life's inspiration with others." This is a free life, and we deserve it.

Once I was doing some consulting for a doctor in Chicago, and we went too late into the evening. We realized that it was about 11:30, so we decided get a bite to eat.

We ended up a little Mexican restaurant, sat down, and ordered something to eat. There were three young men, probably in their twenties or thirties. They looked as if they had been working, maybe in construction.

One of them may have been a year or two older, and he seemed to have a higher position than theirs. He was acting as a senior advisor to the other two. He was giving advice as if he was their leader. He was the kingpin, and they were glued to his advice.

Then two businesspeople came in and sat right next to them. All of a sudden, the gentleman who had been acting as the leader was quiet; he didn't speak. Then somebody came in that was even more powerful-looking than the second two, and they became quiet.

As I watched this game of authority going on, I realized that everybody is a leader to somebody, and everybody is a follower to somebody. So it's unwise to think we don't have leadership skills.

I want you to go in and dig out the treasure of leadership that you have inside. You have it, no matter what level you are playing on or what level you plan on going to. Know that you have leadership, you have the skills, and you have the power. You want to honor them.

One key to leadership is to be willing to embrace both support and challenge. No matter what anybody says about you, you want to be able to say, "OK, that's fine; it serves me." You may be a leader of your family, your school, or your workplace. Whatever it is, you're a leader, and you want to acknowledge it. If you don't, you will minimize yourself and exaggerate the importance of others.

Sometimes people at my seminars put me up on a pedestal. I say, "Listen, I am just a human being. I am just doing what I love doing. My values aren't greater or lesser than yours; they're just different. If you think you see something in me that you admire, stop right now and find out where you have it in yourself, because if you put me on a pedestal, you will minimize yourself. And if you are minimizing yourself, the message I am trying to share is not going to get across. I want you to see me as your reflection. Whatever you see in me you own yourself; discover it and admit it. Otherwise you are an umbilical cord looking for a socket to plug into instead of a human being with your own life and vision. As long as you go around searching for some individual to look up to, you won't look in the mirror and look up to yourself."

I am not negating having a mentor or respecting great accomplishment, which can be extremely useful. But when you find a mentor, understand that what you see in them is inside you. Own it, resonate with them, and draw them into your life. Make a list not only of what they can do for you but of what you can do for them. By fulfilling their values, you can resonate with them and build a great social leadership network. This is what leadership is about. That's the key, because you really do have a leader inside you.

As I watched the gentleman in that little Mexican restaurant first recognize his leadership, then minimize it when he was faced with what he thought was authority, I almost wanted to speak up. I felt like interacting with everybody there and bringing this great lesson to their attention. The first group became quiet, subordinated themselves, and lost their power.

Don't lose your power to anyone. Acknowledge your power. Realize that all the rules we have today are created by people who have power, and whoever has the most power sets the rules.

If you minimize your power and neglect what you are capable of doing, and you don't go out and do something magnificent with it, you may end up attempting flutily to live somebody else's life. You will be living in the *shoulds* and *ought tos* and *supposed tos* of everybody else, instead of the *love tos* and inspirations and dreams that you deserve.

The real treasure of you is acknowledging your inner leader. The real treasure is sitting inside you, waiting to come out. Don't look in the mirror and say, "I don't have it." Say, "I have it," find out where it is, go out, share it, and shine. Be the true, powerful you that you deserve.

Everybody has inherent leadership. They have something unique that's truly their leadership. What is it? What do you want to lead?

I knew early what I would love to offer. I intended to be one of the leading inspirational speakers and educators across the world. I wanted to lead a new movement helping people master their lives and see the order inherent in the universe. But what is it you would love to lead? Everybody has it; they are unique. The more authentic you are, the more it surfaces.

In order to be a leader, you require something to lead, somewhere to lead to, a time to lead, and a reason. When the why is big enough, the hows will take care of themselves. You require a truly inspiring and meaningful reason. What's your reason? How are you going to lead? What do you want to lead? Look to your highest value for the source of such an inspiration.

I've been blessed. In college, I was premed. I was one of the honored students, I achieved great grades, and I was in the premed honor society. I decided I was going to be a chiropractor because I loved the natural healing philosophy. Chiropractic teaches that an innate or inborne intelligence is inside everyone. Everyone has this wisdom of the body, this source of homeostasis. It's only our false beliefs and, misperceptions that interfere with it. If we get our beliefs and perceptions back in order with the laws of the universe, we heal. I love this idea, and that's why I got involved in this profession.

When I graduated, I had the opportunity to speak at my graduation. I said I wanted to be a leader in our profession. I wanted to be able to make a contribution to our profession and keep the inspired philosophy alive in the profession across the world. Today I have the lovely opportunity speak to thousands of chiropractors and other professionals across the world.

I've dedicated myself to that principle because I believe that we are losing sight of the real cause of healing. We think it's an outside job, but the real healer is inside. Sometimes we disempower ourselves, thinking it's out there, but the truth is *here*, inside. If anything out there is working, it's because it has somehow inspired what's within to do its job. There's a power inside us. I wanted to be involved in leadership, and I still speak to a lot of chiropractors and others in the health professions to try to keep that message alive.

If you truly want to make a difference in the world, allow yourself to have and inwardly awaken your global vision. You won't get beyond any of your self-imposed limitations unless you have a vision, a goal, a purpose beyond yourself. Don't let fear and guilt control your life, have something outside you to focus on.

Leadership is expanding consciousness. As Emerson said, our mind is unconsciously constrained by belief systems. As these expand, the mind too expands and is called by your authentic self, or soul to ever greater spheres. Every time we open our heart to see a new vision, a new possibility, a new belief system, we expand our horizons towards infinity.

Would you like to make a difference on this planet, so that when you leave, you can look back and say, "I've done everything I could with everything I was given; I made a difference"? I feel that way. But if you don't define what that is, whom it's for, and what it is going look like, you're leaving it up to the whims of the world and the opinion of others. You're going to be subordinate to their values, instead of taking command and saying, "This is what I commit to doing. And I let nothing on the face of the earth stop me, because this is my mission." Watch what happens when you do that.

It's been my experience that the people who have the greatest cause, the greatest vision, and the greatest dream are the ones that leave their greatness on this planet. When I was seventeen, Paul Bragg said something that stuck with me and has been with me ever since: "If you really want to make a contribution on this planet, which everyone does, deep down inside, think bigger than the planet."

That stuck with me. Then I thought, if you really want to make a difference in yourself, have a vision that is at least as big as your family. If you want to make a difference in your family, have a vision at least as big as your community. If you want to contribute to, and be a leader in, the community, have a vision that is at least as big as your city.

If you want to be the leader of the city, and make some major impact, have a vision and a cause at least as big as a state. If you want to be number one in the state, have a vision and a cause at least as big as the nation. If you want to have a national influence, have a global vision. And the only people I know that have global impact are people with astronomical visions. You influence the sphere that you have transcended in your mind.

It's important to expand yourself. I believe that if we're grateful and a have an open heart, the key of the mind will open with inspiration to take us to the next step. True leadership and social power come when we don't constrain or limit ourselves to small thinking.

We serve the world more by shining than we ever will do by shrinking. As Marianne Williamson said in her book *A Return to Love*, "Our deepest fear is not that we are inadequate. Our deepest fear is that we are powerful beyond measure. It is our light, not our darkness that most frightens us. We ask ourselves, 'Who am I to be brilliant, gorgeous, talented, fabulous?' Actually, who are you not to be? You are a child of God. Your playing small does not serve the world. There is nothing enlightened about shrinking so that other people won't feel insecure around you. We are all meant to shine."

There are seven fears that we sometimes allow to stop us. The first is the fear of perceived authority. We subordinate ourselves to some perceived moral authority that may try to make us feel that we're bad or good or right or wrong and that we could be punished. The ancient oracle at Delphi had an inscription that said,

"Know thyself." I wonder what would happen if we're true to ourselves and let our inner voice and vision be more powerful than the moral or opinions on the outside. The fear of perceived authority can stop us from living amazing lives.

The next fear that stops us is the fear of not being smart enough. The others are fear of failure; fear of loss of money, or poverty; fear of the loss of loved ones; and fear of rejection by people. The last one is the fear of not being healthy or smart or strong or good-looking enough.

If we let any of those fears stop us from our magnificence, we're not going to shine, and we're going to shroud our real potential. We're going to live vicariously through others as spectators instead of participants and empowered leaders.

I don't want to do that in my life. Ever since I was eighteen, I've said that I want to do whatever it takes—to travel whatever distance and pay whatever price—to give my services across this planet. That's how I feel, and I would love for you to feel that way about what you're doing. But if you're attempting to be somebody else and you're trying to live somebody else's life, you won't. Step out of your fears and guilt, and allow yourself a magnificence, a vision, a leadership dream. Go out there and have an astronomical vision of what you can do on this planet. Don't stop with that vision until it's reality.

Some people come up to me and say, "That's nice for young people, but I'm seventy-two years old." But I say, "That's bull. Your age doesn't matter."

In fact, I had a gentleman in Dallas, Texas, who was seventy-two. He came to the Breakthrough Experience and told me that it's for people under sixty.

I confronted him, saying, "So what are you going to do with the next twenty or thirty years of your life? Because if you don't have something to live for, you may have something to die for."

He reflected on that, because his wife had said something similar. Suddenly he became reflective and inspired. About two to three months later, I saw him at another convention. He'd gotten out of retirement, he was dressed immaculately, and he was back in business. He was back in service, using his mind and his talents.

It really doesn't matter where you are or where you've come from. What matters is where you're planning on going and what you're willing to do to get there. Don't let anybody on the face of the earth stop you from what you're capable of doing. And deep inside, you know what you're capable of doing.

Don't let the fears make you lie to yourself, saying you don't know and you can't do it. Don't let anybody who wants to keep you in their small box stop you from going for something grand. You deserve to open up the treasure of grandness, and you have a yearning for a meaningful and immortal effect on this planet.

Don't let anything stop you from that. Don't even let yourself stop you. Focus on your vision and your dreams, and let an inspirational life come to you.

Your vision is what your soul calls you to do, and it's here to lead to whatever it might be. It doesn't matter what arena your highest values are pointing to. When Michael Jordan was asked how he became a great sportsman, he said, "I feel that God put me on the planet to be the greatest sportsman who ever lived." That was his mission.

You may think, "I don't have that kind of vision. I simply want to raise a family." I have a book called *Instantaneous Personal Magnetism* by Edmund Shaftesbury; it's a great book. My copy once belonged to the Kennedy family. In it was written the mission statement of Rose Kennedy: "I dedicate my life to raising a family of world leaders." Who's to say you can't be a mother and raise a family of world leaders?

Ever since I've been a teenager, I've had a dream for myself: to make a contribution in every one of the seven areas of life. When I leave the planet, I want to be able to say that I have influenced the spiritual philosophies and religious organizations of the planet. I believe that there's an inner calling, and it's my grand organized design. It's there in each of us, although sometimes we just don't look within and honor it. Instead we project our values onto others and things, labeling them as good and bad, but in actuality they are just part of a matrix of love, assisting us in being our authentic selves. Some religions say, "God is over here, but not over here, because that would challenge my values." I'm here to look beyond narrowed human evaluations and see a greater order in the world. If I don't see hidden order, it's time to look again until I do. I just keep looking until I discover that it's there.

Sometimes you judge something as terrible, and then, a day or a week or a year or five years later, you find that it actually held something terrific. Similarly, you think some things are terrific, but a day, a week, a month, a year later, you find out they held something terrible. They weren't what you thought. The truth is that it's just the balance of love sitting out there, and you didn't know that you were simply to learn and see beyond those initial assessments. When you look carefully, with the wisdom of the ages, you discover there's nothing but love; all else is illusion. Sharing that is how I'd love to make a contribution spiritually.

Mentally, I'd love to bring transformational methodologies that help people expand their mind capacities and awaken their genius. For my vocation, I'd love to bring methods into the business world to help people to become inspired about their work, because I've developed inspiring methods that achieve this.

Socially, I'd love to make a contribution to those who have global influence and have my ideas and social transformation tools used worldwide. In terms of the family, I'd love to be able to teach the laws that break the myths about family dynamics and ground people on the truth of love. Financially, I'd love to be a financially independent ultrahigh net worth individual bringing forth methodologies for helping people attain their desired wealth. Physically, I'd love to fulfill my mission of bringing methodologies that enhance wellness and wellbeing across the world, and help people realize that love is still the greatest of all healers.

I am making and would love to continue making these contributions to all seven areas; it gives me something to do and keeps me fulfilled and active for my life. Why not? If you have idle time, you plateau. But if you have something to dedicate yourself to for the rest of your life, you become and remain inspired to get more out of your life.

There's no reason you can't be a great leader and leave an immortal effect, awakening the authority inside you, instead of holding on to and depending upon external authorities. As I said, I've taken the time to study the lives of the great leaders. Every time I find something in their lives that matches mine, I grab it, and I write it down. If they can do what they've done, so can I. That's a great affirmation. If Bill Gates can be a billionaire, so can I. If Albert Einstein can leave a legacy in physics, so can I.

Some people say, "That's crazy. That's unrealistic." Not when you're truly dedicated. Many dedicated polymaths have left their marks on history. Find out what you'd love to dedicate your life to. It may be one thing or many things, but find it, lead to it, and go for it. And surround yourself with people that come from that perspective.

What game and playing field do you want to play in? In order to play in that game, just realize that you're going to both please and displease people along the way, just as in family dynamics there's a supporter and a challenger, there's peace and war, and there's cooperation and competition. That's also true in companies and corporations.

If you look at world leaders, you will realize that they have millions of people that condemn them and millions of people that support them. How big are you willing to be. That will depend upon how much challenge and support from others you can handle. If you can have only ten people challenge you before you break down, you're a small leader. If you can have a billion people challenge you and still hold your vision, you're a great leader. The greater the number of people that challenge you, the greater the number of people that will support you. Hold your vision, knowing that it is to be bigger than all the supports and challenges.

Support can build us up, and challenge can humble us and bring us down. To keep in the center, we need both synchronously. A real leader has to embrace both equally. If we see only support, we'll aggrandize ourselves. We will become self-righteous, overproud, and elated with ourselves. This sets us up for attracting challenges, distractions, and maybe even tragedies.

On the other hand, if we listen to all the challenges and negations, we will beat ourselves up. Then we'll find out that people support us and will try to build us back up.

Both support and challenge are equally necessary to keep us focused and centered. Let neither the pleasures nor the pains, neither the support nor the challenge, neither the buildups nor the putdowns, keep us from our mission. Both are feedback mechanisms to help us remain authentic along our journey. Otherwise, you'll be addicted to one and avoid the other. You won't refine yourself into magnificence unless you embrace both simultaneously. If you look back in your life, you'll see that some of the biggest challenges were the things that helped you grow the most. Don't run from them; honor them, and see how they serve you.

Don't addict yourself to support alone, because sometimes support groups alone keep you weakened: they keep you stuck in your fantasy instead of allowing you to break your fictions and get back to practical reality.

A real leader can take on all things from both sides: support and challenge. Embrace them both equally. Whenever you see one, simultaneously look for the other; I guarantee you it will be there if you look carefully. Seeing both, you'll be poised and present and centered. They'll keep you authentic and in your heart, focused on your real objective.

If we become elated with ourselves, we tend to set goals beyond our capacities and in time frames that are too short, leading to self-defeat. Then we'll beat ourselves up. We'll set goals that are too small and time frames that too long. We'll feel accomplished momentarily, but we'll probably continue in this vacillating, oscillating, bipolar condition.

The real master in life knows that support and challenge are two sides of life and come in pairs. Such an individual embraces that paradox, that complementarity of opposites, focusing on the center and the clarity of the real mission. They don't let support or challenge, praise or reprimand, criticism or accolades interfere with their inspired calling.

Once I was at the British Open, walking alongside Tiger Woods. He had a psychologist alongside him to give him feedback. If he shot a magnificent hole and started to feel a little too elated, the psychologist said, "Yeah, but we've still got this many holes left." If Tiger ended up shooting one into the sand trap, the psychologist said, "That means you get to take on the pressure, which is when you do your greatest." The psychologist gave him feedback so he could home in on his authentic self. Take no credit, take no blame; just keep focused on the chief aim, and know that you're a leader.

That's the way you want to start and live your day, embracing both sides of life. That's fulfillment rather than half fulfillment. Embrace both sides of your daily magnet. That's the treasure that sits inside you—the magnetism of opportunity.

We have dreams, we have inspirations, we have value systems, but we may not have the strategies for achieving them. We may have limited our strategies. We've either been too humble or too cocky. We get frustrated. Instead of getting help, searching for new ideas, or expanding our mind, we sometimes hide and lie to ourselves that our goals aren't really important to us. We accept mediocrity instead of allowing ourselves greatness.

Many people who come to me for consultations say, "I don't really want greater achievement. That's not really important to me."

I say, "Well, if I could show you how to more efficiently and effectively have it, would you take it?"

"Oh, yeah."

They'll take it in seconds, but they haven't discovered greater strategies on how to achieve it or given themselves permission to go for what they want. The second they do, they become inspired, and nobody has to get them up in the morning.

There's a difference between motivation and inspiration. Inspiration has to do with something that's so high on your values that you don't even think about not doing it; it's what you love. Motivation involves something lower in your values; it's not inspiring to you, so somebody on the outside has to keep you going.

Leaders find out what is inspiring and are dedicated to doing it. They don't let anybody in the world stop them, and they keep learning new strategies and new methods to keep growing to higher levels.

I believe that we have that quality inside us inherently, and we deserve to let it shine. Find out what's really inside you and give it out to people. Say what you want in return, so you're rewarded for doing what you love. That is one of the most inspiring things you'll ever find.

To be able to get up in the morning, do what you love, get handsomely paid to do it, and enable other people to do the same is what it's all about, as far as I'm concerned.

Over the last fifty years, I have spent tens of thousands of hours researching. I've learned that if you go out into the larger market too soon, before you complete your body of work, you may not get the chance to complete it. I had a dream of completing certain bodies of work before I went out. I've written volumes of material in almost every ology you can imagine. For thousands of hours, I've explored nearly every aspect of human life—anthropology, physics, chemistry, psychology, sociology. I often came across something that would bring a tear of realization to my eye. It sent a chill up my spine, showing me part of the matrix, part of the puzzle of life. I felt it was a revelation, and I thought, "I can't wait to share this with somebody." I found that whatever you're doing, whatever your service is, if you can't wait to give it to people, people can't wait to get it. If your innermost dominant thought is the service that you would love to share, you won't struggle attracting clients. Many nights, I sat in tears, thinking, "It can't be this simple; this is too profound; it's mind-boggling."

When I had moments of this kind, the next day telephones would ring. People would ask for what I'd discovered, although I hadn't announced it yet. There is a nonlocal field of intelligence in the universe, and we are seemingly entangled with every other human on the planet. If we truly get into our heart, honor the leader that's in there, and give our discoveries out in service, I don't believe there's anybody on the face of the earth who can interfere with that immortal dream.

[6]

The Secret and Powerful Treasure of Wealth Building, Financial Independence, and Philanthropic Contribution

Most people have a desire to be financially wealthy. Almost everybody I have ever come across desires to be wealthier than they are. Even if they are wealthy, they want more wealth.

Wealth originally meant *well-being*. We all desire to be whole and well in our being. Now I would like to explore the treasures of wealth, and I want you pay careful attention, because I am about to share something you have probably never heard before.

What if I told you that you already have abundant wealth in your life? You may think, "I don't have a whole lot of cash flow, and I've debts to pay," but I want you to look carefully.

Every human being has a set of values. Whatever's highest on their list of values is the form of wealth that they have. If their highest value is their children, their wealth is in the form of their children. If their highest value is in social interaction and leadership, their wealth lies in their capacity to influence people. If their highest value is in spirituality, their wealth will be their spiritual understanding and influence.

In other words, wealth is never missing in your life, it's just there. But you are probably thinking, "What about paying the bills? I need the cash."

The hierarchy of your values dictates your destiny. If you do not place a high value on cash savings, liquid money, and investing in true assets, your wealth will show up in the things that are more valuable to you. Say the number one thing in your hierarchy of values is your children—their health and education—followed by a beautiful home, vacations, nice clothes, nice furniture, and a nice car. Saving money, building cash, investing in financial assets and having financial independence may be number twenty on your list of values. You will probably have more month at the end of your money than money at the end of your month, because you will spend the money that comes in—no matter how much it is—on things that are higher on your list of values than cash, savings, and investments. You won't have any money for savings or investments, because you will be busy putting it into the things that are more important to you.

It's not that you are missing wealth: it's just not in the form that you are hoping for because you are too busy getting things that you value more.

The first treasure to unfold is that you already have wealth, and it is in the form of your current highest values. You can convert that form back into cash and other financial investments with the questions that you ask yourself. I am not saying to sell your kids, your house, or your spirituality in order to get cash flow or financial wealth. I am suggesting that you first realize that you already have created wealth in your life. You don't lack the capacity to do it; you've just created it in the context of your own values: the highest of your values is the form that it's taking right now.

Honor where you are wealthy now; honor where you are already successful. Once you do, you will realize you already have the capacity. All we are going to do is now is change the form. That's the first treasure you want to get.

If you think that somebody has more wealth than you, you may not be looking at the wealth that you have now. You may have a close and intimate relationship, and no one could pay you a fortune to take that away from you. That's the form of wealth you have.

Let's go to the next step, the next treasure, to help you realize how to convert that form of wealth back into cash in case you would like to have cash flow, savings, and investments. Why would you want to have cash, savings, and investments? Because money is a means of exchange and allows you more options. It is essential to value and appreciate money if we want to convert our present form of wealth into financial wealth.

Our next treasure will show you how to take the value in the wealth that you already have and to convert it into assets and cash flow, so you can have abundance in that form and have more options in your life. This is not to negate what you have now but to diversify it, so you have a greater portfolio of opportunity. Nothing is missing in your life; you are already abundantly wealthy, and you deserve even greater financial abundance.

According to Alfred Marshall in his *Principles of Economics*, you can take your current highest asset or form of wealth and convert it into financial wealth and cash—if you know how to ask the right question. If your highest value is your children and saving and investing money is way down at number ten or more, what you will spend your money on? On things for your children.

What happens if your highest value is saving money and building financial wealth, and your kids are way down on the list? You will end up saving your money and having great wealth, although your spouses and kids will have to take a back seat.

As money comes to you, you manage it according to your hierarchy of values. Let me give you an example. I had the opportunity to consult with a man in Florida who generated $6.29 million in a year. At the end of the year, he had to borrow $327,000 to pay his taxes. How can someone make $6.29 million and have to go into in debt to pay his taxes? Fancy cars, clothes, travel, entertainment, art, and similar things had high value for him; paying taxes and saving money had low value. He had all these possessions, but he didn't have any money at the end of the year.

He had a secretary who made $24,000 a year but saved $400 of that per month. At the end of the year, she had saved more than he did, and she was closer to financial independence than he was.

Financial wealth has little or nothing to do with how much money you make. It has everything to do with how you manage it, and the way you manage it has everything to do with your hierarchy of values.

Let's go on to how you can change your values so you can have the cash flow that you want. Say you discover that saving money and building wealth are number ten or fifteen or twenty on your list of values. Even though you were hoping it was higher, your life demonstrates that it's lower.

Here's what you do: Make a list of how saving money and building wealth could change your life and contribute to the people you care about. Write down not one or two, but 100 or 200 benefits to you and those you care about. If you don't have a big enough reason for accumulating financial wealth, it won't go up high enough on your value list, and you will keep doing what you are doing, expecting different results.

Make this list as huge as you can, maybe even bringing in your family on the project. The more you associate with the benefits, the farther the idea goes into your brain and sticks in your consciousness. You start to see and act on opportunities to achieve what's highest on your value list, whereas you miss out on opportunities and take no action on whatever's lowest. Unless building financial wealth and saving and investing money are high enough values for you, your wealth is going to stay in the form it's already in.

I don't mean becoming infatuated with money or becoming greedy. Those behaviors are for those who have a low value on financial wealth. I am talking about saving and investing it wisely. If you don't save and invest, you will be working for your whole life, and you will be a slave. If you save and invest money, it will start working for you, and you will become its master.

Some pseudospiritual people say, "I'm not in it for the money, and money is not everything." As a result, they're in poverty. They spend their whole lives working for money, and they don't even realize it.

Don't fall into that illusion. Don't separate spirit and matter. Realize that spirit without matter is expressionless, and matter without spirit is motionless. Realize that you want to value money not because it's something to store, but because you can use it to make a difference in the world. You can use it to more effectively serve others, work because you love to and not because your forced to, to live an incrementally greater lifestyle, show what's possible, honor your own magnificence, and raise the standards for all human beings.

Determine your list of values from my website. Then take whatever is highest among them—whether it be your children, your social life, or your spiritual life—and write down how saving and investing money and building financial wealth will help it. Not only are you valuing financial wealth more, but you're linking it to what's important to you now. Ask yourself, how is saving and investing money going to help my children? How will it help me in my spiritual life? How will it help build my business? How will it help me in my social life? How will it help me philanthropically?

If you link financial wealth to what are now your highest values, you won't subtract from your present form of wealth. You'll add to it, because you'll associate it with financial wealth building strategies and will convert it into financial liquidity or cash. Now you'll be able to do what you love and have the abundance to fulfill it in many more ways.

It's been my experience that if you associate with people that have $10, you get $10 ideas and $10 opportunities. If you hang out with people that have $1,000, you get $1,000 deals and $1,000 opportunities. If you hang out with millionaires, you get million-dollar ideas and million-dollar opportunities. The more you save and invest, the more opportunities, associations, and greatness will come into your life.

Write down 100, 200, 300 ways of how saving and investing money will help your life. Link them to your highest values by asking, "How will saving and investing money help me in all the areas that are important to me now?" Do that, and keep doing it. Don't stop;

spend hours, even weeks on it, and I guarantee that you will see moneymaking opportunities that you'd never noticed before.

Here's our next principle: if you don't appreciate financial wealth, you're not likely to acquire it. You may have wealth in many other forms, but if you want it in the form of cash, savings, and investments, you are to value and appreciate these forms of wealth. It's the same in other areas. If you don't appreciate your relationships, they begin to die. If you don't appreciate your clients, they disappear. Whatever you don't appreciate depreciates. If you don't appreciate saving, investments and financial wealth building, financial wealth is not going to come to you. Money circulates from those who value it least to those who value it most.

I've watched people shift their value systems, and in a matter of months, they've changed from being in debt to getting out of debt to saving and building financial wealth. If you'd love to have cash flow and financial wealth, you are wise to value them enough to save and patiently invest your money.

People who say, "I'm not in it for the money" are often lying to themselves. After all, they're spending their entire lives working for money, aren't they? People who devalue money spend their whole lives working for it. People who value it spend their lives saving and investing it, and then it works for them. You're a slave to money if you have to work for it; you're its master if you have it working for you.

The key is to make your piggy bank into your biggie bank. Start with small savings, and incrementally grow your savings and investing and keep building it consistently. Most people don't save because they don't value saving. They think, "When I get a huge chunk of money, then I'll save," but that practically never happens. If you've been waiting and waiting but still haven't started saving, maybe you know what I'm talking about.

Money automatically flows to whoever appreciates it most and knows most about it. You won't study or learn about things that aren't important to you. If you don't value money, you won't study it. If you don't study it, you won't gain knowledge and certainty about it. And whoever has the most certainty rules the game of wealth building and cash flow.

After going through and making those lists and realizing you already have wealth (it just may need to be transformed), it's time find the cause that you're going to use it for. After all, if you don't know what you're going to do with the money, why would the society and the world give it to you? Think about it, if you'd like to have a million dollars, or $10 million, or $100 million, or just $100,000, doesn't matter. If you don't know what you're going to do with it, why would you get the opportunity to have it? The people who end up with financial wealth are the people who know what they're going to do with it. They value it, think it out, and know how to earn, save, and invest it.

Like anything else, whatever you deprecate goes down. So it may be wise to make a decision today: "I'm going to appreciate my wealth and the form it's in. I also appreciate the new form I'm about to create it in. I appreciate the value of money, because it allows people to exchange one form of service fairly and sustainably for another."

If you have zero money saved, and you get your first dollar, that dollar is a 100 percent addition to your savings. If you have $100 saved, the value of that next dollar is 1 percent of your savings. If you have $1,000 saved, it's 0.1 percent; $10,000, .01 percent; $100,000, .001 percent; and if you have $1 million saved, it's 000.1 percent. As you save money, the value of the next additional dollar diminishes, so your motivation to earn that extra dollar starts to decline. Therefore if you don't have an inspiring and intrinsic drive for continuing to grow in your financial wealth, you will eventually plateau. Often people do; they get to a comfort zone and stop. They don't grow, because they don't have a big enough cause.

This is another reason it's important to have a cause, a great mission, in life. If you don't, you'll plateau. You'll start accumulating clutter that will end up running your life instead of managing money because you have a great cause behind it. Think of all the people you can serve in the world; think of the gradually increasing lifestyle you could demonstrate, giving permission for other people to do the same.

Think about this: If I go up to somebody and say, "I'm running out of cash; I can't pay my bills this month. Can you help me out?" they're not likely to help you. If you say, "My teens are about to go to college, and I didn't save and invest so well. I wanted to know if you can maybe help me pay for my college for my teens," they'd say, "Sorry, but I've got my own teens and bills." But consider what happens if you say, "You know, a few months ago, one of the children in our neighborhood was run over going across the busy intersection to the park. I don't want my children to end up in this situation, so we've decided to take the last lot in our community subdivision, and we're going to build a park on this side of the highway so the children in the neighborhood don't have to go across the major street.

"I don't know about you, but my wife and I have decided that we're going to put in our $30,000 to buy this lot, and we're going to make sure that it's turned into a park. I don't know if you'd like to participate—I don't even know if you have children—but if by chance you do and you don't want them to possibly get injured or killed crossing a busy intersection, we'd like to know if you'd like to help us build this park."

When you have a cause that's bigger than you, people join in. So the greater your cause, the greater your potential for financial wealth. The greater the vision you have, the more the people will want to rally and participate in it.

As you grow wealth, you're going to have more responsibility to do something with it. That's why it's unwise to deprecate money, because it demands greater accountability, greater service, a greater vision, and greater social impact. It's a huge contribution to the world to master the art of saving and investing money and building this form of wealth.

Having a cause bigger than ourselves opens up the first key to the great treasure. Don't minimize yourself, thinking you can't do it or you don't deserve it; start to affirm yourself: "I'm a multimillionaire money magnet; everything I touch turns to gold. I deserve the abundance and wealth that is fortunately surrounding me."

Start thinking and talking that way. Live every day humbly asking your inner voice and vision to guide you to ever greater causes and uses for your wealth. And watch the abundance flow into your life.

I have a friend who created a foundation for paralyzed children. When he started it, he was a teenager. Now the foundation has millions. Millions of dollars passed into the hands of a teenager because he had a cause, a vision, an inspiration. He valued himself enough to declare what he wanted to do. This increased the wealth potential not only for him but for his foundation.

Bill Gates is a multibillionaire partly thanks to Microsoft Windows. Why is he a billionaire? He created something that has impacted and is used by a billion people. Can you see that he has created something that's worth that much?

What is your cause? What is your contribution? What service that you could uniquely offer that millions or billions of people could use? I believe that way down inside you is something original that's worth that amount, but you are responsible for drawing it out of yourself.

Ask, what do people need? What talent or service or product do I have that could fill that need? I wonder what would happen if you were to ask yourself that question and didn't stop until you came up with an answer that was worth $1 billion. Dig deep, and explore until you find something that you know you can contribute.

We deserve to share our gifts or services with the world and be rewarded for it. But it is equally as important to pay and reward ourselves fairly and to declare to ourselves and others that we are worth it. No matter what you have done or not done, you are worthy of love. You are worthy of economic rewards and abundance.

Some people think, "When I get an extra amount, I will start to save and invest. Right now, I've got too many other bills." They're valuing everybody and everything else first and minimizing themselves. That's why they pay themselves last. It's been my observation that the financially wealthy pay themselves and their greater cause first.

In fact, I had a great lesson about this. Many years ago, I started my speaking career in my little apartment when I was going to professional school. I invited people over for these little classes. I put a little bowl out on the counter, which said, "Love donation."

I gave a talk for two to three hours. I thought it was inspired. I thought I did a great job, but at the end of it, only one individual put any money in the little bowl—$5.

I thought, "This isn't going to cut it; I will require much more to make a living and pay for school here. So I put a note on the bowl that said, "Minimum donation $5." The next week, I got two or three $5 bills.

"That's still not going to cut it," I said. "I am not going to be able to pay my bills with this." Then I wrote, "$10 minimum love donation." I got a few more $10 bills, and I think I made $30. This was still not going to cover it, so I realized I had to push them further. I put a note out that said, "Minimum donation $20."

The same thing happened. Finally, I got frustrated and said, "I deserve more than that." And I wrote,

"Minimum *fee* $20." The moment I did, 85 percent of the people that came to the little talk (about twenty) put their $20 in there. I was astonished. The universe was waiting for me to declare I was worth something. It was almost as if people didn't know what to pay until I declared it. All that was required for me to do was declare that I was valuable and I had something to say.

If you keep waiting for others to decide your worthiness for financial wealth, you are going to wait for eternity, because nobody's going to get up in the morning to help you attain your financial magnificence. It's up to you. It's time for you to acknowledge your magnificence and your wealth and say you are worth it. The best way to do that is to pay yourself first.

That was one of the greatest turnarounds for me in my financial life. Once I learned that, I started asking for what I felt was a fair exchange and saving a portion. I did forced automatic saving, because I noticed that my emotions were getting in the way of saving. I said I wanted to save a certain amount, but I started thinking, "Maybe I can't do it" and hesitated. I went to a financial brokerage company and had them automatically take the savings out of my business account. I did not missed the money after that; somehow enough came in to cover my bills. The moment I started to save, my financial destiny changed. It seemed the more I saved and eventually invested, the more money came.

I can't emphasize the importance of just doing it. Go to a bank or brokerage company and set up a forced saving and then investment plan so you don't have think about it again. Don't waver; don't emotionalize. Money is built with strategies, not emotions; by actions, not hesitations. All you have to do is save and eventually invest; there's no real risk in it. The worst that can happen is that you may occasionally be tempted to pay your bills with the money that you save. But don't give in to those temptations. Save anyway, and figure out how to do more service and get more creative to make more income. Find a way. Go the extra mile for people, and watch what happens. When you start to manage money wisely, you get more money to manage. One of the greatest things you will ever do is to pay your savings first and then your investments.

The second thing to do is pay your taxes. Pay your lifestyle third, and pay your business bills last (if you own a business). Pay them all by priority. When money is managed by priority, more money comes in. When money is managed wisely, more flows in. Whoever has the most certainty—and you have certainty when you have your saving and investments forced— gets the cash flow.

Prioritize all your expenditures, because people who prioritize their bills manage their money more wisely than those who don't. By prioritizing, I mean put your bills in order, and pay them starting with the ones that penalize you most down to those that penalize you least.

When you are trying to start to save money, remember that if you do not initiate the incremental savings process, waiting for the big kill, it's not necessarily going to happen. Start with little amounts and gradually build them up. Start small and build big instead of waiting for the big turnaround.

When I first started saving years ago, I was kicked in the butt by a lady who worked in my office. She disappeared for a weekend, got married, came back, wanted her paycheck, and moved to a different city. Here was a girl who had worked for me for just a few weeks. She disappeared over the weekend, came back, wanted a last paycheck in advance, and gave notice— and here I was, paying myself last. This was when I first opened up my business, playing the altruist, lying to myself, having a hidden agenda, saying, "I'm not in it for the money." I was frustrated, having more accountabilities, more debts accumulating. I finally said, "Damn it, that's not the way I want to work it here." I started to pay myself first. That was the day my financial wealth building began.

I went over to a brokerage house and made an electronic commitment. I didn't know if I could afford it, but I just did it. I started off with $10 a day: $50 a week, $200 a month. You probably think, "That's not a lot. He's a doctor," but that was a stretch for me. I was afraid to do it, because I had debts, I was behind on bills, and I had excuses for why I couldn't afford to pay. But when I put an automatic savings in place, I didn't miss the money at the end of the month. Somehow an little bit extra came in to cover that.

A few months later, I increased my savings to $300. Another few months went by, and I realized, "I am not missing that money. It's not interfering with my lifestyle: I am still doing everything I plan to do, and I am getting an extra few patients." I raised my savings to $500, then to $700 and $900, and broke the $1,000 mark. At that point, I was starting to see new possibilities. I saw that after fifty years I might have financial independence. Then I moved my savings to $1,100 a month, then, three months later, to $1,210 a month, then three months later to $1,344 a month. I kept increasing it.

At the end of the year, I realized that I hadn't been saving for my taxes. I was angry, because I had to take money out of my savings account and give it to the government. I didn't like that.

I got smarter. I said, "OK, first comes me; I'm going to pay myself first. Second, I'm going pay my taxes." I had that amount taken out automatically as well. I started paying myself first and my taxes second.

At the end of that year, I had all my taxes caught up, I had my savings in order and accelerating, my business went up to compensate, and I saw light at the

end of the tunnel. By the end of that year, I was saving almost $1,500 a month. I thought, "Wait a minute
now. This is starting to kick into gear." So I decided
that every time I got comfortable, I would kick up my
savings, because it seemed to be working.

So about every three months, I made the habit of
raising my savings by 10 percent. If I'd been saving
$1,000 for three months, I'd bump it up to $1,100.
Three months later, another 10 percent—$1,210. I kept
pumping it up 10 percent every quarter. As I did, more
business came to me, more opportunities, and more
people wanted to take me to lunch and dinner.

It's interesting. When you've saved $100, you get
$100 opportunities; when you've saved $1,000, you get
$1,000 opportunities; when you've saved $1 million,
you get $1 million opportunities. Would you agree that
Bill Gates get billion-dollar opportunities on a daily
basis?

Every time you save and then invest, you get the
benefits of doing so, such as compound interest. But in
addition, new ideas, new associations, new opportunities to show up. Geometric compounding that opens up
the doorway for greater financial wealth. So I started
my immortality account, because my goal was to have
my money make more money than I made by working; I wanted to have a passive income exceeding my
active income. That way, I wouldn't work just because
I had to, but because I loved to.

At first, it was slow. I did a projection every quarter. I would stop and ask, "OK, how much do I have saved?" I would run projections for the next five, ten, fifteen, thirty years to see where I would be if I kept at that rate and accelerating it. When I looked at that in comparison to my lifestyle, I could more or less predict when I would have financial independence.

I learned another principle. I put in a checks and balances system: every time I wanted to raise my lifestyle, I had to raise my savings and my tax payments by the same amount. If I wasn't willing to do that, I wasn't ready to raise my lifestyle. Before, I'd been raising my lifestyle without raising my savings and investments; then I'd be burdened by my lifestyle. So I said, "OK, if I'm going to raise my lifestyle by $1,000, I'm going to put an extra $1,000 in savings or investments, and an extra $1,000 into taxes."

Next, I put together a budgeted lifestyle: this is what my lifestyle is, here's what it is per month, and I live within this budget. If I raise it, I also raise the amount of savings, or investments and taxes as well. If I do that, I will get more money to come in. I can't explain it, except it works. If you do that, you end up increasing your income amazingly.

If you're working on a fixed income, you won't need to do that within just a few years, because as you start saving and investing money, you start feeling more entrepreneurial, receiving opportunities and ideas, and contacting people who think in business terms. You have more courage to go out and do your own thing, and you're soon in your own business. Or you get promotions or opportunities to make more money, because your creative mind is thinking along those lines.

As you save and invest, run projections. Imagine where you will be one year from now if you saved and invested that amount consistently once a month. Then imagine where you will be years and decades from now. That will give you an incentive to push yourself further. Once you see your money grow, you become inspired by your financial potential, and you want to make sure that nothing interferes with its growth.

When you bought your first house or car, you probably wondered, "Can I afford this?" After about three months of making payments, you found you could. It worked. You were able to afford it. Then you got comfortable again. You plateaued, you kept making the same amount of money, and your income stopped growing.

What would happen if, instead of stopping at that comfort zone, you pushed yourself a little further and every three months you increased your savings and investments by at least 1 percent, if not 10 percent? Let's say you're saving $100 a month. At the end of three months, you raise it to $110, and so on. People can tolerate 10 percent changes without too much emotion. So if you're saving $100, and you go to $110, you don't overreact, but you do save. If you just add a little bit more each quarter, once you get comfortable, and once you get used to the savings process, you'll be looking forward to that growth.

Once you start to force-accelerate your savings and investments, mastery of money begins. You're setting up a strategy that builds great fortunes. You'll see the magic of how your intention and your creations can change the universe around you.

The real secret treasure is sitting inside, but maybe you haven't applied the principles that make it surface. Use a forced accelerated savings and investment technique. Then the magic that occurred in my life to bring me where I am today will happen for you. You deserve a vast fortune.

If you have a cause and you know what you are going to do with it, you can allocate some savings and investments for that cause. But make sure that you yourself are in there; make sure that you are actually part of that cause. If you do, you will live an amazing life, and you'll be able to make major contributions to this planet.

I guarantee you if you start this process, eventually you will no longer be on a fixed income. Within two to three years, you're going to be in a different position. You're going to give yourself permission to run your own company or get more promotions and have compounding passive income. By then you'll have learned that the more value and service you provide, the more you deserve. You'll realize that there's no such thing as a fixed income unless you have a fixed belief system. So accelerate the savings and investments, and watch the magic begin.

Build a good financial cushion—at least three to six months of capital. You'll stabilize your business as well as your personality, because a reserve of money stabilizes your emotions. When you don't have any money in reserve, you are more likely to be highly volatile. When you have large capitalization, you are stable, and you make wise decisions.

The more money you have, the more people will want to give you money. People will come up to you and ask, "Can I pay you to spend some time with me? Is there any way, I can buy your lunch?" Sure. Whenever somebody buys your lunch, find out how much it costs, take that amount and put it in savings, because if you were planning on buying yourself lunch, you believe you can afford it. Force it into savings or investments, watch what happens, and watch more people take you to lunch. The wealthier you are, the more free lunches you get. That's a savings program in itself, as long as you save the difference.

Make sure to build in financial cushions for your wealth. Save, build a stabilizing cushion, and keep buying conservative investments before you go to riskier ones. Don't speculate with your money before you've invested it; don't invest until you have some foundation of savings in place. Preserve your principal before you take risks. You don't need to take huge risks with money to build financial wealth. There's a science to building wealth. Saving is the most significant initial component.

[7]

The Secret and Powerful
Treasure of an Inspired
Mission, Presence,
Equanimity, and
Enlightened Awareness

W e're about to open up the next secret treasure: your inspired or spiritual mission. Whether you're aware of it or not, you have probably been on a spiritual quest all your life. In all areas, there's a calling to immortality. We may desire to have a life after life, or to at least have our mind and our ideas leave some effect through history. We have a desire to keep our career or business from dying before we do, or pass it on to offspring or buyers. We want to it carry on beyond our lifespan. We want to have more money at the end of our life than life at the end of our money. We want our relationships and our family to live beyond our lifetime, and we want to be known and remembered socially for our unique and lasting contribution. We'd also like to have the Fountain of Youth and live immortally as an inspired and vital body.

There's a yearning inside all of us for something beyond our daily lives, for some immortal component. We have a spiritual quest inside us, whether we are aware of it or not.

Our spirituality is also influenced by our hierarchy of values: everybody sees their spirituality according to their own highest values. In other words, if your highest value is your family and your children, you will see your spiritual quest as raising a magnificent family, like Rose Kennedy. A person running a business may see their spiritual mission as running great businesses and giving excellence service. As we've seen, Michael Jordan saw his purpose as being a great sports figure.

We don't want to lock ourselves into thinking that our spirituality consists only of going to church, a synagogue, a mosque, or a temple, or meditating, chanting, or praying, because then we will be limiting spirituality to a little box.

I'd love for you to explore the possibility that your spiritual life is just as magnificent as anybody else's. Mine may be traveling the world, setting foot in every country as a teacher, healer, and philosopher. I feel like that's my special spiritual contribution. Whatever it means to you, it's OK: that's your spirituality. Don't box it in or judge another individual for theirs, because they're going to express their spirituality according to their highest values. They're no more or less spiritual than you.

Many world conflicts are caused by the boxes that we put ourselves and others into, thinking our form of spirituality is greater or lesser than theirs. That alienates instead of integrates. It stops us from loving and puts us into the mechanism of "I'm right, you're wrong," and "I'm better, and you're worse." This creates exclusivity instead of inclusivity.

Realize that every human being is expressing their spirituality according to their own highest values. If an individual's highest value is wealth building, who's to say that that's not their spiritual quest? Who's to say they're not going to make a great and inspiring contribution? Once at the old Mayfair Hotel in New York City, I was sitting with a billionaire who was dedicating his energies to funding the Tibetan Foundation and supporting the Dalai Lama's mission. Somebody later that day said to me, "I don't believe in materialism and all that wealth building stuff. I don't think that is spiritual; that's the opposite of spiritual."

Yet most of the billionaire's money was dedicated to what he perceived to be a spiritual quest: it was for a whole culture that he had his spiritual mission. Sometimes we can't see that spirituality has no boundaries. It is an expression of what inspires people most.

Maybe if we dug deeper into our own secret treasures inside our hearts, where love lives, we might realize that everything is worthy of love. No matter what you've done or not done, you're worthy of love. I believe that's the key to spirituality: to be grateful for our lives and for other people, and to love ourselves and other people for their own hierarchy of values and uniqueness.

When I was studying morals and ethics, I learned something fascinating: somewhere in the world is your opposite. Whatever you stand for, somebody else will stand against. You both grow from it. So don't box in your spirituality with rigid absolutes. One individual's heaven could be another individual's hell. Honor everybody else's form of spirituality and realize that they have their own set of values and their own spiritual quest. That furthers your spiritual quest, because somebody's is required to play their side in order for you to play yours. Everyone has spirituality inside in their own unique form and expression. Let's honor it, let's embrace it, let's learn from it.

Once I was in El Salvador, and I saw a group of people going to a funeral. They were celebrating and cheering. They were wearing white and blue and other colors. They were celebrating the passage from a mortal body into a spiritual domain.

"Wow!" I thought. "What a totally different way of conceiving of a passing compared to another culture, which may see death as a doomsday!"

I want to learn from all the different forms of beliefs, because that expands me instead of contracting me. True spirituality is more inclusive than exclusive and reaching towards the infinite, not the finite.

Let's realize that our spirituality is just as great as anybody else's, but let's also honor theirs as well as ours. Let's see the spirituality that permeates the world and allow it to express its great treasure as a great love. Love is the elegant and beautiful synthesis and synchronicity of all complementary opposites.

For many decades, I've had a desire not only to live but to understand health, well-being, and human potential. That's been my life. I have a mission book that goes wherever I go. I update it on my computer every day. It contains my mission statement and my dreams and long-term objectives. It presently totals thirty-three volumes. It contains every single goal and objective that I would love to create in my life—spiritually, mentally, vocationally, financially, socially, physically. I've spent more time on this mission book than on anything else in my life, because I've found that once my mind is clear and my heart is into my mind's clarity, magical synchronicities occur: the world opens up doors for me. If my mind is not clear, I am faced with working ever harder to achieve my objectives.

I will spend an hour or two hours or even a half a day on one paragraph of this book, reading and refining it until I get a guiding and confirming tear of authenticity and gratitude in my eye. The only entries that go into this book are things that inspire me. I don't want anything that doesn't inspire me, because I want to live an inspired life. This book contains what I want to accomplish while I am alive and after my passing over the next thousand years. I keep records of all the goals and objectives that I set out to do and have accomplished, all the things that I didn't expect, and all the blessings that come in my life. This is my life. This is what I do. Everything is dated.

Weeks, months, or years from the moment I write down these things, they start to manifest. You won't be able to convince me that writing down your dreams is not powerful. You can see it in my mission book; it's there, it's live. I've found that it works, and I encourage you do the same. Define how you would love your life to be, spiritually, mentally—in every area. Doors open up for whatever we write down as our spiritual path.

What is your inspired or spiritual mission? What is your service to the world? What do you want to contribute? What is your hidden spiritual agenda? What do you want back?

Nearly every weekend for thirty-three years, I have presented a seminar program called the Breakthrough Experience. People ask me why I keep doing this program, because it's not in large groups. It's just moderate sized workshop groups.

I love sitting before people who are opening their hearts, communicating their love and appreciating to some individual, or in some cases to themselves, over actions they previously judged and resented. I have the opportunity to sit there with tears in my eyes just as they do and be before a group of people in moments of their authenticity. I'm getting to be with authentic people in a moment when they're not cocky or humiliated; they're humble to the previously unseen hidden order and expressing certainty in a moment of grace. I believe it is a gift to be able to live day after day watching people be authentic, break through, and discover their and other people's magnificence. That's my spiritual reward. Not only do I get economic rewards, but I get the spiritual fulfillment of watching people be authentic, seeing possibilities for themselves and breaking through limitations and judgments.

When you've almost died (as I have), and then later have the opportunity to learn and develop inspiring new methods for human transformation, you feel you have been given a torch that can awaken and inspire others. When you have a clear internal drive to fulfill this mission, you just want to get into action and serve. When you've found this, and you accumulate insights and further refinements on how to fulfill this mission even more effectively as you go along, then you just want to help people in even a more reproducible way. How could you not?

On a weekly basis, I've watched people open their hearts and love those they had not been able to love, sometimes for days, weeks, months, or years, including themselves, and break through their fears and guilt. I've also watched them look in the mirror and say thank you to themselves.

People say, "Why don't you retire?" Screw retirement. Retirement is for people who have not found their mission. My heroes are people like the ninety-four-year-old lady who climbed Mount Kilimanjaro—the people who find their dreams, who are dedicated and inspired. They go out, and they don't let anybody on the face of the earth stop them. Those are the people I love to associate with. Find that spiritual mission; find what really inspires you.

You've heard of mindful meditation or grateful prayer as a method of spiritual expression. I would like delve into that, because I believe that everyone down deep inside has the opportunity for inner communion.

We are surrounded by opinions all over our life. Almost everybody we meet has some opinion to tell us and is projecting their values onto us. That's great: we can learn from everyone with a different mindset. But sometimes it's wise to go inward and listen to our own inner voice and see your own inner vision. I have been probing that possibility for many years, and I've found some real treasures.

It's been shown that when our mind is in a state of balance and we see the order around us, we feel gratitude. Gratitude is the key that opens up the gateway of the heart and allows the love that's eternally present to come out. When our heart is open with gratitude and love, our mind becomes clear and inspired. Then a vision, an inner voice, an inner message come to us, and our body becomes enthusiastic and ready to act on the vision and those messages.

On a daily basis, maybe as you get up in the morning, it's wise to stop before you get out of bed and think about what you are grateful for. It takes no effort to be ungrateful, but it takes reflection to mindfully see the things you can be grateful for. I guarantee that every single day of your life, there's something to be grateful for. Stop, reflect, look, pay close attention, identify it, and think about it. As you do, you will start to feel a welling up inside, and you will start to appreciate your life and the people in it. The moment you do, close your eyes, and lie (or if you want, sit) in silence.

Now that you are grateful, go inward and imagine talking to your inner most authentic self: "All right, inner self, what vision do you have to reveal to me today? What message do you have for me? What guidance do you have?" I cannot tell you how empowering it is to do this.

In a state of true gratitude, suddenly the inner voice is revealed, and the inner vision is clarified. You really can become inspired by this. To me, this is a communion within. You might say that meditation is like listening to this inner voice and seeing this inner vision. Prayer, if you will, is like talking to it. You have an inner dialogue with your innermost being. This will guide you, because in this state of gratitude, you will receive creative insights and then take magnificent actions. Some of the greatest music, poetry, art, and ideas have emerged this way. Even great new business ideas. Do this on a daily basis, before getting out of bed. Have a notepad next to your bed so you can write down your insights or priorities for action. I encourage you to do this every day. I also suggest that you do this at lunch right after you have eaten. After a nice meal, sit, reflect, and do the same exercise. Maybe do the same thing before you go to bed.

If you practice being grateful, you will have more things in your life to be grateful for. You cannot plant flowers in the garden of your mind without having more flowers grow. The more we look for things we can be grateful for, the more things we will receive to be grateful for.

To me, gratitude is the key that opens up the spiritual quest. When the internal voice and vision become greater than all external opinions, you have begun to master your life. This is where leaders, original thinkers, and geniuses are born. This is true spirituality—communication with the inner vision and message. Do this daily.

Many of the world's spiritual traditions and perennial wisdom sayings were born out of individuals who took the time to do this. Sometimes we subordinate ourselves to other, supposedly more spiritually aware, individuals instead of following in their footsteps and trusting our own inner vision and voice. These are not dissociated crazy voices of distress and instability. This is the inspired voice, the inspired vision, the one to guide your life by. I have used it for many years, and it has allowed me to do things that I would never have been able to do without it.

In 1901, a Canadian psychiatrist named Richard Maurice Bucke published a great book called *Cosmic Consciousness*. He studied the forty-three of the most illuminated people in history and found that what they had in common was this very act: going into a state of gratitude, going inside, getting silent, having a dialogue with their inner self, and using that to lead their lives.

This is awakening your spirituality on another level. This is digging the deepest you can into the secret treasures you have inside. It bestows a brilliant, shining radiance on you. When people see you, they are amazed, because there's something different, something special about you. Do this daily. Watch what happens. Your life will never be the same.

There's a hidden order in your life. If you haven't looked for it, I invite you to join me, because I can show you how to see it. The moment you do, I guarantee your life will no longer be the same.

I offer a course called Synchronicity. In it I take your age, whatever it is, and divide it up into quarters: one quarter for each half day.

Let's say you're forty-eight. On the first day, you look at everything you can remember in the first twenty-four years of your life. In those years, looking moment by moment, you get truly present and see if there's any moment when somebody was nice to you without somebody else being mean, or when somebody was mean to you without somebody being nice. See if there was any praise without reprimand, any rejection without acceptance, anybody taking something without giving something. You job is to become so fully conscious and present that your unconscious mind is able to intuitively reveal the equal and opposite sides, the positive and the negative, in any moment of perception. If you make a list of every moment you have perceived to be one-sided, you can find the equal and opposite if you become present. When people do that, they're brought to tears, because they discover that they haven't had a one-sided event. They just thought they did. Perceptions are made of contrasts and each memory simultaneously has an anti-memory to balance the electronics in the brain.

When you realize that, you understand that fear of the future is an illusion. Fear is an assumption that in the future you're going to experience more pain than pleasure, more loss than gain, more negative than positive. Yet you have no true evidence from your childhood that that has ever occurred. It can't, because the world within you and around you is maintaining balance. When you understand that truth, fear and fantasies dissolves.

Guilt is an assumption that you have caused more loss than gain, more negative than positive, more pain than pleasure, for somebody or yourself. But again, if you truly become present and fully conscious in the moment, you realize that when you've been mean, somebody else has been nice, and when you've been nice, somebody else has been mean. There's an equilibrium, an equal and opposite reaction. When you understand that, you know there's no reason to deprecate or inflict guilt on yourself. You realize, "No matter what I've done or not done, I'm worthy of love, and the same is true of other people." You realize there's a matrix of love on the planet, although we rarely take the time to look for it. I'm dedicated to helping people look, because I guarantee you with inspiring certainty that it's there.

People say, "I just want to be happy," but happiness is a mask that covers up the true love that's in your heart. Happiness is an addiction which breeds sadness to compensate. True love is a profound, illuminated, enlightened state. It's not transiently excited; it's poised. It's powerful, it's clear, it's lucid, and it transforms lives. At the moment when my mother loved me, she wasn't happy, and she wasn't sad. She was love. I don't think there's anything grander than a mother's love when she shares it in that depth.

I believe that there is a quantum field of love in the world. Like the electromagnetic field of light (and like all things), it has two sides. If we don't take the time to look for those sides, we'll project our values onto it, and we'll see it either supporting or challenging us; we won't see it as loving us. We attempt to separate them, although they're inseparable in actuality. They're separable for our minds, but inseparable to the hearts that knows. We have to look beyond our polarized emotional mind, into our heart, to see this great truth. When we do, we have equanimity, and we automatically have gratitude. We don't have to shift anything.

As stated previously, gratitude is the key that opens up the gateway of the heart. When the heart opens automatically, love is sitting there, waiting to come out. Deep inside every child loves its parent; every parent loves its child and is waiting for the day when they can finally express it.

Remorse, bereavement, or grief over a death is due to infatuation with the loved one. When you truly love them, they're you won't feel their loss. They're present with you, you feel their presence, and you have love with them. You can walk around day or night and have access to them. When your heart is open, the miracles of love are born; magic is awakened. (Of course, a miracle is really a natural law put into operation; it's just called a miracle by people who don't understand the laws.)

Gratitude clears and releases the receiving and broadcasting system of the mind. Consequently, the body becomes enthusiastic, and you become present. When you have the four cardinal pillars of self-mastery, gratitude, love of the heart, certainty, and presence of mind, I don't think there's anything on this planet that can't be summoned into your life. We're here as intentional creators, to create matter and add energy to manifest forms. Whoever has the most is able to manifest the forms most effectively; whoever has the most self-worth manifests the most directly.

We have access to these creative powers. That's our spiritual quest: to cocreate in the world, to transform things into what inspires us. If you can see the order on the outside, you're the one that has the order, and you reveal it from the inside.

About 1973, I was sitting on the floor of my parent's house, and I picked up a great book by the seventeenth-century German philosopher Leibniz. It was a discourse on metaphysics, a philosophical dissertation on the religious principles of the world, and I was fascinated by it. At the time, I was studying everything I could that could help me expand, because I had learning difficulties and I wanted to catch up. I came across this book, which said something that changed my life.

The first chapter referred to "Divine Perfection." If you're not religiously oriented, imagine the divine as a permeating intelligence in the universe, possibly what physicist David Bohm described as the implicate order in the universe. If you're religious, imagine it being the grand organized design. In any case, imagine that there is a field of intelligence or order that permeates our life. If we look deeply enough, we'll discover it. Leibniz said that there is a divine perfection, divine beauty, divine magnificence in our lives and in everyone's lives, but few people come to know it. They live in mediocrity. For those that do know it, their lives are never the same; they have changed forever.

Ever since I read that, I've wanted to know what this hidden order is. It was Albert Einstein who said (I'm paraphrasing), "It is enough for me on a daily basis to sit and explore and contemplate the great intelligence that permeates and governs the ordering laws of the universe. I just want to know how this intelligence works. I want to know his mechanisms of operation. I want to know the natural laws."

I believe that deep inside us, there is a yearning for finding order in the apparent chaos of our lives, and I believe it's there. For fifty years, I have dedicated my life to unveiling it. And I believe that's what the Demartini Method does: help people see the hidden order in their apparent chaos.

Reading great, inspired pieces of work changed my life, and I encourage you to do the same. I don't know what that means to you. It may be reading a book by a great football player, or a religious work, or a biography of a leader or artist, even a business or social leader. In any case, surround yourself with the most inspiring pieces of literature you can get your hands on.

Put your hand into the pot of that glue. Read every day, even if it's just a passage. Find some writer filled with inspiration; fill your day with their thoughts. Don't just read it and set it aside. Write those quotes or phrases down. When you do your gratitude exercise, go to your own inner voice, and get a revelation, write it down as well. Accumulate these and create a book of inspirations. You can turn to it whenever you have a less than inspired moment in your life.

I've created a book called *The Philosophers of Wisdom*. I have extracted the greatest teachings that I could get my hands on. I have put my hand in that pot of glue, and it's stuck with me, allowing me to have a more inspired life.

We deserve that kind of life. Our real brilliance emerges when we fill our minds with such radiance. Read great, inspired writings, from no matter what source. Fill your mind with these ideas daily. Take ten to fifteen minutes every day; you don't have to read more than a phrase.

My grandmother was an amazing lady. I went jogging with her when she was ninety-seven years old. She was 101 when she passed away. Every day she read proverbs and psalms and lived an inspired life partly because of it. I'm not saying you are to read those same particular pieces; just find something that inspires you.

I'm living an inspired life because I'm filling my mind with great and inspiring ideas. If you want to live an inspired life, surround yourself with inspiring people. If you're not able to meet them individually, read their literature on line, or read their books. Tomorrow you'll be the same individual you are today, except for the people you meet and the books you read. Fill your mind with great ideas.

Create a library of inspiration, and watch what happens. I guarantee you that inspirational reading changes lives. I've gotten letters from around the world that said, "Your books inspired me; they've changed my life."

Make that your life. Take some of my books, or other books, fill your mind with them, and watch what happens. Your life will not be the same. My life has never been the same since I did that at age eighteen.

You are also wise to look at whom you associate with. I wrote down that I wanted to interact, associate, and even co-teach with some of the greatest spiritual teachers on the planet.

When I was in Nepal, I was looking in a bookstore, reading some books on the Bön religion, the original teaching of the Tibetans. The man in the bookstore said, "You seem very serious about studying this body of teachings."

"Yes, I'm studying comparative religions," I said. "I'd love to study this body of teachings too."

"I have a book for you. Hold on one minute." He went to the back and pulled out a very old text.

I read it for three or four hours and took notes. The man said, "You're very dedicated. No one ever takes time to do this."

"Yes," I said. "I want to compare all the religions, philosophies and sciences of the world and find the common thread in all of them. If we focus on what's common, we grow in love; if we focus on what's different, we tend to judge."

"The leader of this religion, the Bönpo Lama, is here in Kathmandu. My brother works with him; he's in the monastery."

He asked me if I would love to meet him.

I said, "I would love to."

"I'll call him on my cell phone."

The Bönpo Lama said he could see me. I sat with him for an hour, talking about philosophy and theology and listening to his teachings.

He said, "Maybe you can help spread the message of my faith across the world." He gave me every volume that he'd ever written. They helped me carry them down the hill to a rickshaw, and I took them back to my hotel.

I'd written it down in my state of my mission goal and objective book: "I'd love to meet the great spiritual teachers of the planet." If I could meet the Nobel Prize winners, why not the spiritual teachers? Why not the great entrepreneurs? I got to meet Paul Allen, cofounder of Microsoft, and Richard Branson, when we launched Spaceship I in the Mojave Desert in 2004.

There are amazing people on the planet; just allow yourself to meet with them. Harmony lies in diversity, which gives you certainty. When you have certainty about your mission for humanity, you resonate with people that also have such certainty.

Read what inspires you. Make a list of people you'd love to associate with. Read that list every day, and watch how synchronously you will be at the right place at the right time to meet them. They'll be sitting next to you on a plane; you'll be in a restaurant where they'll show up there.

I wrote down fifty names of world impacting individuals and celebrities that I wanted to meet. I've met them now. I've also gotten to meet another two thousand plus people that I envisioned and dreamed about meeting.

When you read something and think about it, you resonate with it, and you show up at the right place at the right time. If you're in business and your innermost dominant thought is about clients, you resonate with it, and it becomes yours. Clients come to you. What you seek seeks you.

The hidden order in the universe is hidden not because it has to be, but because we haven't taken the time to look. We're so busy with our daily routines that we don't stop to listen to the field of intelligence that permeates and inwardly guides us.

I've built a question into the process of my Breakthrough Experience. When, say, somebody criticizes you, you ask, "OK, where are you criticized? Who perceives that in you?" Don't be self-righteous about it; own it, 100 percent. Then broaden your mind and find the balancing benefit to you, because if you look carefully, when somebody criticizes, somebody else is praising you. This is all a process of equilibration. There's no criticism without praise. Though the two poles may be non-local. And both are simply holding you accountable to be your most authentic and loving self.

I've seen this repeated over and over again, and I am certain that it's a perceptual law. It was called the law of simultaneous contrasts by the father of psychology, Wilhelm Wundt. Those involved in this synchronous balancing act may be one or many, male or female, close or distant, virtual or real, but they're there. One is trying to lift you up; the other is trying to bring you down. They're trying to keep you in homeostasis, like a chemical redox reaction in a cell. Our society generates a redox reaction to keep us in our hearts. If we only see the praise, we become elated; if we see only reprimands, we get depressed about ourselves.

If we become addicted to pleasure, it is because we are denying its opposite side; if we become "subdicted" from the pain, we are again denying the other unconscious side. If we can't see the downside, we become infatuated; when we can't see the upside, we get resentful. But in actuality, both are occurring.

If we see both of these sides synchronously, we enter into a world that the great psychiatrist Carl Jung called *synchronicity*. Synchronicity is living in an acausal timeless state. If we see one side without the other, we live in *dichronicity*: living through time, which ages us.

Usually you don't take the time to look. As a result, you emotionally react to almost anything. You either resent or become infatuated; you don't see the balance. You carry this emotional baggage into your life. Unless it's equilibrated and freed, it will weigh you down to the grave. When it is equilibrated, it liberates you by turning into light, enlightening your mind. When you see both sides at the same moment, you have an enlightened mind. In that moment, you realize that you are neither reprimanded nor praised; you're loved, because love is a synthesis and synchronicity of attraction and repulsion, praise and reprimand, nice and mean, kind and cruel.

In thousands of cases, people think they are being abused or treated violently. If you look carefully at the same moment in their lives, they also had somebody, locally or nonnocally, who was overprotecting, overnurturing, too soft on them. The overprotector and the overviolent one were a team of two, working together to make love. We revolted against one and became addicted to the other. The more we became addicted to one, the more the other one came in to break us of the addiction and wake us up to the truth of love. There's a hidden order the whole time. If you look, family dynamics is loaded with such equilibrium.

In our society, our addiction is the idea that we're supposed to have one side without the other. We're supposed to be nice and never mean; kind, never cruel; sweet, never bitter; positive, never negative. Life is not that way, but we have this fantasy that it will be someday, when we're perfect, but that's not going to happen. This illusion obscures the magnificence of what's already here. Right here, the praise that supports is balanced by the reprimand that challenges. This makes you independent. Otherwise you are dependent. You require both in order to maximally grow.

No matter what you've been through in your life, nothing out there can stop you except you. You deserve to have your dreams, and you deserve to follow these great seven secrets and treasures in your life.

You can have these treasures in your life come to the surface; you can shine; you can glimmer; you can have brilliant facets in your life; you can have what you love. You won't convince me otherwise. I'm living proof of it. I share it with you, and I would love for you to do the same. When you do, I would also love for you to find me and share your inspiring story, so that I may be able to share it with somebody in the future. May your seven secret treasures live on for the rest of your life.

ABOUT THE AUTHOR

Dr. John Demartini is a human behavioral specialist and founder of the Demartini Institute, a private research and education institute dedicated to activating leadership and human potential. He's an international author and business consultant, working with CEOs of Fortune 500 companies, celebrities, and sports personalities. Globally, he's worked with individuals and groups across all markets, including entrepreneurs, financiers, psychologists, teachers, and young adults, assisting and guiding them to greater levels of achievement, fulfillment, and empowerment in all areas of their lives.

For more information about Dr. John Demartini, his live events, and range of products and services, contact the Demartini Institute on info@drdemartini.com. To view our website, visit www.drdemartini.com.

CPSIA information can be obtained
at www.ICGtesting.com
Printed in the USA
JSHW050020300722
28722JS00004B/4